Practice with Spreadsheets

100+ Easy-To-Follow, Real-World Exercises

Sandra T. Myers, M. Ed.
The Chubb Institute

100% Classroom Tested and Approved

Prentice Hall
Upper Saddle River, New Jersey 07458

Aquistions Editor: Carolyn Henderson
Assistant Editor: Audrey Regan
Editorial Assistant: Lori Cardillo
Executive Marketing Manager: Nancy Evans
Project Manager: Lynne Breitfeller
Senior Manufacturing Buyer: Paul Smolenski
Manufacturing Coordinator: Lisa DiMaulo
Manufacturing Manager: Vincent Scelta
Cover Design: Jill Yutkowiz
Editing and Interior Design: Mark R. Meyers

A Simon & Schuster Company
Upper Saddle River, New Jersey 07458

ISBN 0-13-456682-3

Prentice-Hall International (UK) Limited, London
Prentice-Hall of Australia Pty. Limited, Sydney
Prentice-Hall Canada, Inc., Toronto
Prentice-Hall Hispanoamericana, S.A., Mexico
Prentice-Hall of India Private Limited, New Delhi
Prentice-Hall of Japan, Inc., Tokyo
Simon & Schuster Asia Pte. Ltd., Singapore
Editora Prentice-Hall do Brasil, Ltda., Rio de Janeiro

Printed in the United States of America

10 9 8 7 6 5 4 3 2 1

Dedication

I would like to dedicate this book to the best family in the world: my husband, Rich, and my children, Mark, Maria and Krista. Thank you for all your support and patience and thanks to my brother, Joe, for all his help. I would like to especially thank my many dedicated students for all they have taught me. Their encouragement inspired me to write this book.

Spreadsheets Exercises
Table of Contents

The last two exercises in each unit are Concepts Summary Exercises and are a review of the entire unit. Grids are provided for these exercises. An extra grid is included at the end of the book. These exercises also can be used as tests or to review for tests.

Cross-Reference

Directory of Files

Name of File	Exercise
ANALYSIS	111
ANTIQUE	86
AUTO	84
AUTO2	85
BASEBALL	5, 12, 23, 37, 59, 66
BENEFITS	107
CARS	9, 13, 28, 31, 38, 90
CHARGES	17, 25
CHECKBOO	106
COMMISS	40, 49, 80
COMPUTER	109
DOCTOR	34, 81
DOLLS	82, 93
DOLLS2	98
ENGLISH	54, 75
EXPENSES	7, 43, 57, 73
FAMILY	97
FLOOD	110
FORECAST	105
FRUIT	8, 18, 29, 50
FUND	96
FUND2	99
GRADES	4, 11, 30, 76

Name of File	**Exercise**
INCOME	19, 32, 58
JEWERLY	53, 70
JFK	91
JFK2	92
LUIGI	6, 16, 20, 27, 39, 60
MUSIC	33, 41
MYBUDGET	14, 48, 61, 68
PAYDAY	103
PAYDAY2	108
SALARY	26, 44, 51, 63, 67, 74, 89
SHOTS	62, 83
TRAVELOG	104
VACATION	10, 69
VENDOR	3, 15, 24
WEDDING	42, 45, 52, 77
WYLIES	102

Use this cross reference page if you are missing information in retrieved files or to locate files. Beginning with Unit 3, the last two exercises in the units are Concepts Summary Exercises. The Concepts Summary Exercises are reviews of concepts learned in the unit and are unique exercises. They will not be retrieved and are not listed in this cross–reference.

Introduction...

Electronic spreadsheet programs are one of the most popular and common software applications used today. Their widespread use has created a demand for trained employees at all levels.

Most spreadsheet software applications work basically the same way, and this book can be used for the "hands–on" approach to most electronic spreadsheet applications currently on the market. The sequential lessons in this book were developed in a logical progression from simple to more complex concepts that kept in mind different levels of comprehension. Most PC instructors believe that the "hands–on" approach aids in the comprehension and clarity of computer concepts.

The models in each exercise are taken from "real–life" electronic spreadsheets used in many different types of business, personal, and educational settings. The most frequently used concepts in the business world are given added emphasis.

Each of the 14 units focus on several objectives and each unit has several exercises with step-by-step, easy–to–follow directions. The student creates the models to obtain the desired end results by applying the several concepts focused on in each lesson. The units build new concepts while mastering previously learned ones. Two Concepts Summary Exercises are included at the end of each unit (except Units 1 and 2). The concepts learned from the unit will be applied in these Concepts Summary Exercises. A grid (columns and rows) is included in each of these Concepts Summary Exercises for the students to write labels, values, and formulas, thereby developing the spreadsheet model.

I collaborated with many of my colleagues and discovered most of them agreed that monitoring students in their formula development, especially in the introductory and intermediate classes, provides an excellent base for the student's comprehension of basic and more complex formulas. Students are encouraged to write formulas in the book. Not only will this aid in the development of formulas for the students, but it also will permit the instructor to monitor and preview the formula development on hard copy while at the same time giving the student later reference.

I wrote this book at the request of many students. After having taught electronic spreadsheets in a corporate and educational setting for years, I have discovered that the same questions are asked again and again by each new group. From these questions, I developed the "Helpful Hints" sections. These "Helpful Hints" not only will answer the questions "most asked," but they also will aid the instructor in his or her lecture or class presentation.

Students should read *all* instructions and "Helpful Hints" *before* beginning each exercise. Each new unit also provides a unit page as a review of concepts introduced in that unit. Students also should pay special attention to the unit page.

I hope those learning electronic spreadsheets will find this book to be interesting and beneficial.

Practice with Spreadsheets

100+ Easy-To-Follow, Real-World Exercises

UNIT 1

Concepts:

Introduction
Electronic Spreadsheet Uses
Parts of the Screen
Moving around the Spreadsheet
Cursor Movement

Points to Remember:

- Electronic spreadsheets are extremely powerful and are used in most corporate environments.
- What you see on the screen is a very small part of the spreadsheet. It is like looking at your town in relation to the entire world.
- The blank arrangement of rows and columns allows the user to build a model.
- Using the exercises from this book, you will create models that mirror real life situations.
- A model contains three elements: labels (words), values (numbers to be calculated) and formulas (mathematical calculations).
- Most spreadsheet programs combine features of spreadsheets, databases and graphics.
- These exercises are developed to be used with most electronic spreadsheet software programs.
- Lessons are developed sequentially so that models will be created and later retrieved to be used in developing more advanced spreadsheet models.
- At the end of each unit (except units 1 and 2), the user can review all concepts learned in that unit with Concepts Summary Exercises. These will not be retrieved.

Exercise 1- Introduction, Uses of the Electronic Spreadsheet

An electronic spreadsheet is an arrangement of horizontal rows and vertical columns used to do financial or numeric analysis. They can solve almost every type of problem that involves numbers and calculations.

To create a model you usually follow these steps: start the software application, enter labels (words) and values (numbers), enter formulas (mathematical calculations), sometimes explore "what ifs"(changing values to change end results), save the model, print, and quit the program or create another spreadsheet.

This exercise book will follow the above steps. In the first several units you will be entering labels and values and then as you retrieve your models, you will add formulas and functions (short cut formulas). On some models, you will change values to explore "what ifs." After entering formulas, you will save your model, print it and then continue to create models or quit.

These exercises are taken from common "real-life" models used everyday in the corporate and personal environments.

The following are common uses of spreadsheets:

- calculating payrolls
- comparing costs, profits, and prices on products
- forecasting sales
- comparing wholesalers
- calculating prices and discounts
- predicting expenses
- projecting profit
- budgeting personal expenses based on income
- averaging grades
- calculating loan payments
- calculating and comparing salespersons' commissions
- inventory

Spreadsheets have become an important tool for numeric analysis, accounting models, and financial statements. Understanding spreadsheet terminology is crucial in the comprehension of any electronic spreadsheet software.

Directions

Start your electronic spreadsheet application and look at your screen. Study the terminology on the next page. Try to find a column, a row, a cell, the cell address, the tool bar, etc. Due to the software, version, and operating system, your electronic spreadsheet screen may differ.

SPREADSHEET SCREEN

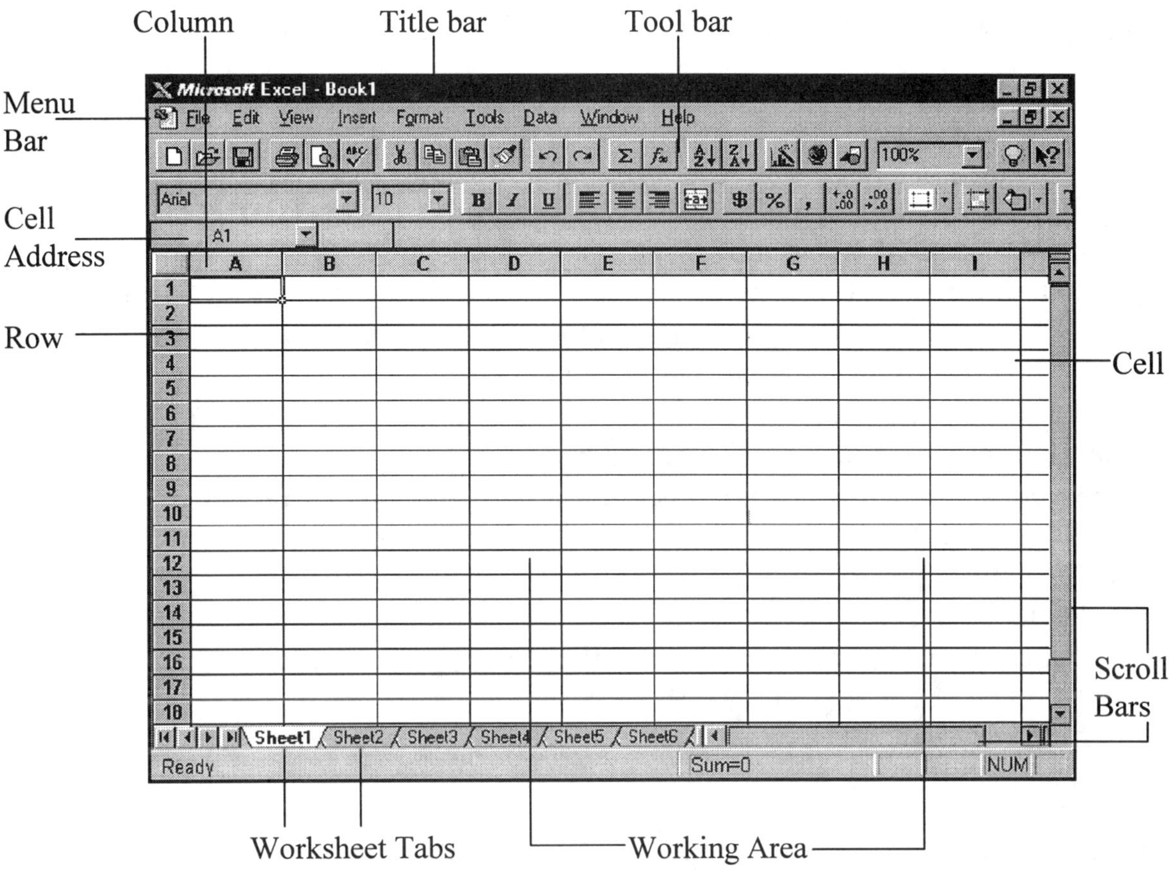

Screen Elements	Description
Column	Vertical (think of columns on a house). Columns are usually lettered starting with A and continuing to Z, then AA, AB, etc.
Row	Horizontal (think of rows in a theater) and numbered consecutively.
Cell	Intersection of a row and a column.
Cell Address	The column letter first and then row number. Example: C7, A9. Cell addresses usually appear in the upper left side of the screen.
Working Area	This is where the models are created. The screen shows a very small part of the entire working area.
Worksheet Tabs	Scrolls from one sheet to another.
Scroll Bars	Scrolls through your document.
Title Bar	Illustrates the software and file name.
Menu Bar	List of available commands.
Tool Bar	List of icons.

Exercise 2 - Moving around the Spreadsheet Cursor Movement, Directional Keys, Go to Key, Home

Directions

1. Open a new blank file and look at your screen. Compare it to the picture in the previous exercise and find the following: Column, Row, Cell, Cell Address, Title Bar, Scroll Bar, Tool Bar, Menu Bar, Working Area and Worksheet Tabs. Some or all of these parts may be present on your screen.
2. Put the cell pointer in A1. Press your right arrow key three times. Look at the upper left of your screen for the cell address.
3. Press your down arrow key six times and watch your cell address change.
4. Go to A1 the fastest way.
5. Use the Goto key to go to cell Z1000.
6. Go down one page.
7. Go to the right one page and then back to A1 the fastest way.
8. Use the Goto key to go to DZ7289.
9. Go to A1.
10. Go to cell A2955.
11. Press your TAB key. What did it do?
12. Hold down your CTRL key and press your right arrow key twice. What did it do?
13. Go to A1.
14. Go down 4 pages and then go to A1.
15. Click your mouse on cell A1, hold down your left mouse button, and drag down to highlight column A—from A1 to A20.
16. Deselect (unhighlight) that area by clicking off of the selected text.
17. Using your mouse, highlight columns A, B, C, D, and E by clicking and dragging on the frame.
18. Deselect the columns and go to A1.
19. Go to the *last* cell of the spreadsheet.
20. Using your mouse, highlight rows 1 through 10. Deselect the rows.
21. Highlight the entire worksheet with one click. Deselect the area.
22. Highlight four rows at one time. Now deselect it.
23. Go to A1.
24. Type in your first name but do not press Enter. Notice that your name does *not* go into the working area of the screen until you press Enter or click another cell.
25. Press Enter and look at your screen. Where is your cursor?
26. Go to the cell with your name and press the Delete key.

UNIT 2

Concepts:

Entering Labels
Entering Values
Changing Column Widths
Naming and Saving the File

Points to Remember:

- Labels are text or numbers not to be calculated.
- Values are numbers, formulas or functions entered into cells to be calculated.
- The *first* character entered determines the status of the cell–whether it is a label or a value.
- Values default to right align and labels default to left align in their cells.
- When a label in a cell is longer than the cell is wide, labels will spill over into the cell at the right. Values *cannot* spill into the next cell.
- Never clear the screen unless you have first saved the file (spreadsheet).
- When you are inputting several spreadsheets into the computer at once, follow these steps in order: create the spreadsheet, save the spreadsheet, clear the screen or close the file, and then create the next spreadsheet.
- To make corrections while keying in entries, backspace incorrect characters *before* entering.
- Look at your screen as much as possible and use HELP when you are in doubt as to what to do next.
- The cell address is the column letter first and then the row number. Example: A7, B3.

Exercise 3 - Entering Labels, Naming, Saving Files

SAVE AS: VENDOR

Vinnie Masterson recently opened a vending business and will need to order supplies on a month to month basis. He needs to keep a total record of sales for each month in the first quarter.

HELPFUL HINTS

- ➔ Always be aware of the location of your cell pointer.
- ➔ The contents of the cell (labels) will align to the left. This can be changed in later exercises.
- ➔ Proofread for errors and correct by backspacing before you enter.
- ➔ Because this book can be used with several different electronic spreadsheet software programs, your screen may appear different.

Directions

1. Enter the spreadsheet exactly as shown.
2. Type FRESH DAILY VENDORS in cell A1 and press Enter.
3. Type FIRST QUARTER in cell A2 and press Enter.
4. Enter the file name and exercise number on each spreadsheet as in cells A14 and A15.
5. SAVE AS: VENDOR.

	A	B	C	D
1	FRESH DAILY VENDORS			
2	FIRST QUARTER			
3				
4		HOT DOGS	PIZZA	PRETZELS
5				
6	Jan.			
7				
8	Feb.			
9				
10	March			
11				
12				
13				
14	VENDOR			
15	EXERCISE 3			

Notes:

Exercise 4 - Entering Labels, Saving, Naming Files

SAVE AS: GRADES

As a junior, Krista Beaumont thought it would be a good idea to keep a record of her grades for each semester. This will allow her to monitor her performance to be aware of errors in her grades and to later calculate her averages.

HELPFUL HINTS

➔ When you enter the heading in cell A1 and A2, you *do not* have to widen column A.
➔ When saving the spreadsheet, always save by file name. Do not use the exercise number.
➔ Depending on your computer's operating system, some file names can have only eight characters.

Directions

1. Enter the spreadsheet exactly as shown.
2. Proofread and immediately correct errors.
3. Enter the label, FIRST SEMESTER GRADES in A1. Its contents will spill into the empty cells to the right.
4. Also enter the label, JUNIOR YEAR -- 1995 in cell A2. It will also spill into the empty cell.
5. SAVE AS: GRADES.

	A	B	C	D	E
1	FIRST SEMESTER GRADES				
2	JUNIOR YEAR -- 1995				
3					
4	COURSE	TEST 1	TEST 2	TEST 3	TEST 4
5					
6	ENGLISH				
7					
8	HISTORY				
9					
10	SPANISH				
11					
12	PHYSICS				
13					
14	CALCULUS				
15					
16	BIOLOGY				
17					
18					
19	GRADES				
20	EXERCISE 4				

Notes:

Exercise 5 - Entering Labels, Saving, Naming, Changing Column Width

SAVE AS: BASEBALL

The Northeast regional manager will be ordering shirts, pants, hats and gloves for their six little league teams. The northeast manager will be taking an inventory of items needed for each team.

Directions

1. Enter the spreadsheet exactly as shown.
2. Enter the title, LITTLE LEAGUE INVENTORY in cell A1.
3. Enter MAY, 1995 in cell A2.
4. Change column A to a width of 11.
5. SAVE AS: BASEBALL.

	A	B	C	D	E
1	LITTLE LEAGUE INVENTORY				
2	MAY, 1995				
3					
4	TEAM	SHIRTS	PANTS	HATS	GLOVES
5					
6	BLUE JAYS				
7					
8	CARDINALS				
9					
10	HAWKS				
11					
12	EAGLES				
13					
14	FALCONS				
15					
16	RAVENS				
17					
18					
19					
20	BASEBALL				
21	EXERCISE 5				

Notes:

Exercise 6 - Entering Labels, Saving, Naming Files, Changing Column Width

SAVE AS: LUIGI

Luigi has decided to redecorate Luigi's Homemade Pasta Palace. He has compiled a list of items that he needs before he can begin operations in his newly decorated restaurant.

HELPFUL HINTS

➔ Check cell addresses carefully when entering labels.
➔ Check for accuracy.

Directions

1. Enter the spreadsheet exactly as shown.
2. Type LUIGI'S HOMEMADE PASTA PALACE in cell A1. It will spill into the empty cells.
3. Type NEW REMODELING INVENTORY in cell A2.
4. Change column A to a width of 11.
5. SAVE AS: LUIGI.

	A	B	C
1	LUIGI'S HOMEMADE PASTA PALACE		
2	NEW REMODELING INVENTORY		
3			
4		COST PER	NUMBER OF
5	ITEM	ITEM	ITEMS
6			
7	PLATTERS		
8			
9	NAPKINS		
10			
11	CREAMERS		
12			
13	PLACEMATS		
14			
15			
16	LUIGI		
17	EXERCISE 6		

Notes:

Exercise 7 - Entering Labels, Changing Column Width, Saving, Naming Files

SAVE AS: EXPENSES

The Sweets Candy Company is starting to gather its data for Projection of Business Expenses for its first year in business. The company will add to this projection as its business grows.

Directions

1. Enter the spreadsheet exactly as shown.
2. When typing in information in cell A1, type PROJECTION OF BUSINESS EXPENSES in A1.
3. Type SWEETS CANDY COMPANY in cell A2.
4. Set column A to a width of 20.
5. SAVE AS: EXPENSES.

	A	B
1	PROJECTION OF BUSINESS EXPENSES	
2	SWEETS CANDY COMPANY	
3		
4		
5		
6	EXPENSES	YEAR 1
7		
8	RENT	14567
9	UTILITIES	1198
10	MACHINERY/ UPKEEP	1010
11	SALARIES	387000
12	ADVERTISING	8235
13	DELIVERY/FREIGHT	1500
14		
15		
16		
17	EXPENSES	
18	EXERCISE 7	

Notes:

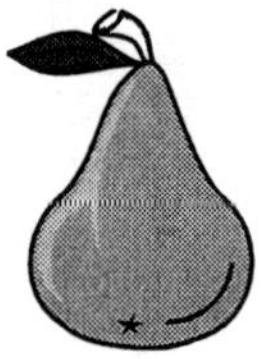

Exercise 8 - Entering Labels, Changing Column Width, Saving, Naming Files

SAVE AS: FRUIT

John's fruit stand has been quite successful. He has been purchasing all of his fruit from a wholesaler in the city. John will eventually want to compute his total sales.

Directions

1. Enter the spreadsheet exactly as shown.
2. Enter JOHN'S FRESH FRUIT in cell B1.
3. Enter WEEK ENDING JULY 16, 1995 in cell B2.
4. Set column A for a width of 12.
5. SAVE AS: FRUIT.

	A	B	C	D
1		JOHN'S FRESH FRUIT		
2		WEEK ENDING JULY 16, 1995		
3				
4			AMOUNT	COST
5	PRODUCT	UNITS	SOLD	PER UNIT
6				
7	BANANAS			
8	PLUMS			
9	PEACHES			
10	CHERRIES			
11	PEARS			
12	KIWI			
13				
14				
15				
16				
17				
18				
19				
20	FRUIT			
21	EXERCISE 8			

Notes:

Exercise 9 - Entering Labels, Changing Column Width, Saving, Naming Files

SAVE AS: CARS

Bill's A-1 Used Cars keeps records of the monthly sales of each salesperson. Bill can use this spreadsheet at a later date for employment information or bonuses.

HELPFUL HINTS

➔ Press Enter after each entry. Type the data and use your arrow keys or your mouse to go the next cell.
➔ Make sure to save the file by its file name and not the exercise number.

Directions

1. Enter the spreadsheet exactly as shown.
2. Change column A and C to a width of 11.
3. SAVE AS: CARS.

	A	B	C	D
1	BILL'S A-1 USED CARS			
2	SALESPEOPLE REPORT			
3	FIRST QUARTER			
4	TOTAL CARS SOLD			
5				
6	SALESREP	JANUARY	FEBRUARY	MARCH
7				
8	PILIO			
9	COCHRAN			
10	GUNKLE			
11	BELL			
12	LOMBARDO			
13	ULLMAN			
14	SULLIVAN			
15	SHADE			
16	WESTON			
17	ASSOUSA			
18	KLOPP			
19	PARKER			
20				
21				
22	CARS			
23	EXERCISE 9			

Notes:

Exercise 10 - Entering Labels and Values, Changing Column Width, Saving, Naming Files

SAVE AS: VACATION

Vanessa Chenault has decided to take a vacation. She is starting to gather data on vacationing in Bermuda or Jamaica.

HELPFUL HINTS

➔ Values will right align in their cells.
➔ Labels will left align in their cells and the columns will not look balanced. You will change this later.

Directions

1. Enter the spreadsheet exactly as shown.
2. Change column A to a width of 12.
3. SAVE AS: VACATION.

	A	B	C	D
1	VANESSA'S CRUISE			
2				
3	BERMUDA			
4				
5	ROOMS	ONE DAY	TWO DAYS	
6				
7	ECONOMY	489	639	
8	STANDARD	534	684	
9	DELUXE	579	729	
10	SUPER	606	756	
11	MAGESTIC	640	790	
12				
13	JAMAICA			
14				
15	ROOMS	ONE DAY	TWO DAYS	
16				
17	ECONOMY	532	732	
18	STANDARD	587	787	
19	DELUXE	623	823	
20	SUPER	658	858	
21	MAGESTIC	711	911	
22				
23	CRUISE			
24	EXERCISE 10			

Competencies:

After completing this unit, you will know how to:

1. Enter labels and values
2. Save a file
3. Name a file
4. Change column widths

UNIT 3

Concepts:

Retrieving Files
Resaving and Replacing Files
Changing Column Widths
Aligning Labels
Editing with Overtype
Editing with the Edit Key
Erasing Cell Contents

Points to Remember:

- In some software programs it is necessary (or a good idea) to clear the screen or close the file before retrieving a spreadsheet.
- When resaving and replacing files, the *new* and revised spreadsheet saves over and replaces the *old* spreadsheet. Be careful to change the exercise number on the spreadsheet when resaving.
- When widening a column, make the column one space wider than the widest entry.
- When entering values in the thousands, do not type the comma.
- For a value to display correctly, the cell must be *one space wider* than the *value itself*.
- Values with decimals that end with zeros after the decimals will round to the nearest number and drop off the zero or zeros at the end. Example: 8.50 will round to 8.5.
- To use the overtype method, simply go to the cell with the error and retype the new information.
- To delete data in a cell, highlight the cell and press the Delete key.
- When using the Edit key, press the Edit key and then look at the upper left of the screen. Use the Arrow keys in conjunction with the Insert and Delete key to make changes and then Enter.

Exercise 11 - Retrieving, Entering Values, Changing Column Width, Resaving, Replacing Files

RESAVE AS: GRADES

Krista has completed four tests in each subject.

Directions

1. Retrieve GRADES.
2. Enter the values in columns B, C, D, and E exactly as shown.
3. Change column A to a width of 12.
4. In A20, change EXERCISE 4 to EXERCISE 11. Simply retype the information.
5. RESAVE AS: GRADES.

	A	B	C	D	E
1	FIRST SEMESTER GRADES				
2	JUNIOR YEAR -- 1995				
3					
4	COURSE	TEST 1	TEST 2	TEST 3	TEST 4
5					
6	ENGLISH	98	100	91	88
7					
8	HISTORY	92	90	87	86
9					
10	SPANISH	97	85	89	90
11					
12	PHYSICS	99	98	100	100
13					
14	CALCULUS	100	90	95	91
15					
16	BIOLOGY	85	87	100	100
17					
18					
19	GRADES				
20	EXERCISE 11				

Notes:

Exercise 12 - Retrieving, Entering Values, Aligning Labels, Changing Column Widths, Resaving

RESAVE AS: BASEBALL

The baseball manager has collected the data for his little league teams.

HELPFUL HINTS

- ➔ Be careful when resaving and replacing a file with the same name. The original file is overridden by the new file.
- ➔ Values will right align in their cells.
- ➔ Labels can be right, left or center aligned.

Directions

1. Retrieve BASEBALL.
2. Enter the values in the spreadsheet exactly as shown.
3. Change the widths of columns B, C, D, and E to eight spaces.
4. Center the column headings in A4, B4, C4, D4, and E4.
5. In A21, change EXERCISE 5 to EXERCISE 12.
6. RESAVE AS: BASEBALL.

	A	B	C	D	E
1	LITTLE LEAGUE INVENTORY				
2	MAY, 1995				
3					
4	TEAM	SHIRTS	PANTS	HATS	GLOVES
5					
6	BLUE JAYS	23	21	23	9
7					
8	CARDINALS	25	25	26	9
9					
10	HAWKS	22	23	24	10
11					
12	EAGLES	21	21	22	9
13					
14	FALCONS	27	26	25	10
15					
16	RAVENS	27	26	25	11
17					
18					
19					
20	BASEBALL				
21	EXERCISE 12				

Notes:

Exercise 13 - Retrieving, Entering Values, Changing Column Widths, Resaving

RESAVE AS: CARS

Bill would like to record the number of cars sold each month by each salesperson for the first quarter.

Directions

1. Retrieve CARS.
2. Change the widths of columns B and D to 10 spaces.
3. Enter the values in the spreadsheet.
4. Adjust the exercise number in cell A23.
5. RESAVE AS: CARS.

	A	B	C	D
1	BILL'S A-1 USED CARS			
2	SALESPEOPLE REPORT			
3	FIRST QUARTER			
4	TOTAL CARS SOLD			
5				
6	SALESREP	JANUARY	FEBRUARY	MARCH
7				
8	PILIO	12	15	9
9	COCHRAN	5	9	15
10	GUNKLE	18	19	18
11	BELL	11	12	10
12	LOMBARDO	22	19	20
13	ULLMAN	13	14	12
14	SULLIVAN	21	24	23
15	SHADE	15	15	5
16	WESTON	19	18	17
17	ASSOUSA	15	16	16
18	KLOPP	17	22	27
19	PARKER	15	17	19
20				
21				
22	CARS			
23	EXERCISE 13			

Notes:

Exercise 14 - Entering Labels and Values, Column Widths, Saving, Naming Files

SAVE AS: MYBUDGET

You have made a New Year's resolution to get organized and you feel that developing a personal budget is a good place to start. You begin your budget by entering your income and expenses into an electronic spreadsheet.

HELPFUL HINTS

➔ Leave rows 5 through 9 blank.
➔ When you save this spreadsheet, be sure to make the file name MYBUDGET one word.
➔ As you enter labels and values in the bottom half of the spreadsheet, top parts of the spreadsheet may not be visible on your screen.

Directions

1. Enter the spreadsheet exactly as shown.
2. Widen column A to 23 and column E to 11 spaces.
3. Narrow columns B, C, and D to 5 spaces each.
4. SAVE AS: MYBUDGET.

	A	B	C	D	E
1	MONTHLY BUDGET FOR MONTH OF				JANUARY
2					
3	INCOME				
4	MONTHLY PAYCHECK				2011
5					
6					
7					
8					
9					
10	EXPENSES				
11					
12	MORTGAGE				475
13	CAR PAYMENT				236
14	GAS FOR CAR				55
15	TELEPHONE				49
16	WATER				39
17	SEWAGE				30
18	CABLE				25
19	ELECTRIC				109
20	VISA				80
21	MASTERCARD				140
22	LACY'S				60
23	INSURANCE--HEALTH				290
24	DOCTOR BILLS				45
25	DENTIST BILLS				0
26	WAGE TAX				22
27	INSURANCE--HOUSE				280
28	OTHER				79
29					
30					
31	MYBUDGET				
32	EXERCISE 14				

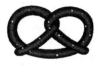

Exercise 15 - Retrieving, Aligning Labels, Column Widths, Erasing Cells, Resaving

RESAVE AS: VENDOR

Vinnie's business has started to expand and he has added new products.

HELPFUL HINTS

➔ Column width can be changed before or after you type the data.
➔ Centering column headings will help the appearance of your spreadsheets.

Directions

1. Retrieve VENDOR.
2. Retype JANUARY, FEBRUARY and MARCH in cells A6, A8 and A10.
3. Change column widths as follows:
   Column A -- 10
   Column B -- 10
   Column C -- 7
   Column D -- 11
   Column E -- 13
   Column F -- 13
   Column G -- 11
4. Enter the column heading SANDWICHES in cell E4.
5. Enter the column heading HAMBURGERS in cell F4.
6. Enter SALAD in cell G4.
7. Center the headings in B4, C4, D4, E4, F4, and G4.
8. Erase cells A1 and A2 and type the heading FRESH DAILY VENDORS -- FIRST QUARTER in cell B2.
9. Center all labels in column A.
10. Enter all values in spreadsheet. Check for accuracy.
11. Adjust the exercise number.
12. RESAVE AS: VENDOR.

	A	B	C	D	E	F	G
1							
2		FRESH DAILY VENDORS -- FIRST QUARTER					
3							
4		HOT DOGS	PIZZA	PRETZELS	SANDWICHES	HAMBURGERS	SALAD
5							
6	JANUARY	212	289	431	303	190	270
7							
8	FEBRUARY	290	329	449	360	266	340
9							
10	MARCH	320	354	457	377	321	367
11							
12							
13							
14	VENDOR						
15	EXERCISE 15						

Notes:

Exercise 16 - Retrieving, Aligning Labels, Column Widths, Erasing Cell Contents, Resaving

RESAVE AS: LUIGI

Luigi realizes that he needs to purchase more inventory for his remodeling.

HELPFUL HINTS

- ➔ You will change the width of each column in this spreadsheet.
- ➔ In cell B17, the tablecloths actually cost $9.50 but the zero will drop and not show on the spreadsheet.

Directions

1. Retrieve LUIGI.
2. Delete cell contents in A16 and A17.
3. Change the columns widths as follows:

   Column A -- 20
   Column B -- 12
   Column C -- 13

4. Center all the column headings.
5. Enter all new information (labels and values) in the spreadsheet.
6. Enter LUIGI in A26 and EXERCISE 16 in A27 as shown.
7. RESAVE AS: LUIGI.

	A	B	C
1	LUIGI'S HOMEMADE PASTA PALACE		
2	NEW REMODELING INVENTORY		
3			
4		COST PER	NUMBER OF
5	ITEM	ITEM	ITEMS
6			
7	PLATTERS	22.55	45
8			
9	NAPKINS	2.35	100
10			
11	CREAMERS	5.67	50
12			
13	PLACEMATS	5.75	50
14			
15	SUGAR BOWLS	5.67	15
16			
17	TABLECLOTHS	9.5	35
18			
19	TABLE PADS	11	30
20			
21	SALAD BOWLS	4.56	15
22			
23	CANDLEABRA	45.55	25
24			
25			
26	LUIGI		
27	EXERCISE 16		

Notes:

Credit

Exercise 17 - Entering Labels and Values, Saving, Naming Files

SAVE AS: CHARGES

Zak Johnson has several charge cards and is on a limited budget as a college student. He uses these charge cards for books, clothes, shoes and personal items while he is away at the university.

Directions

1. Enter the spreadsheet exactly as shown.
2. Adjust column A width to 12 spaces.
3. Adjust column B width to 13 spaces.
4. SAVE AS: CHARGES.

	A	B	C	D
1				
2	ZAK'S CHARGES			
3	FIRST QUARTER			
4				
5	CHARGE	ACCOUNT NO.	BALANCE	PAYMENT
6				
7	ZISA	12-99-9821	309	120
8	J.S.GOODS	45-90-8788	187	60
9	COSMO	65-87-2332	97	45
10	LACY	76-98-9899	24	24
11	ALBERTO	23-23-2322	65	65
12	THE RAP	11-32-2997	15	15
13	COLEMAN	33-98-3433	120	30
14	DRY GOODS	24-87-8789	54	30
15	PENS, ETC.	99-76-9898	80	80
16				
17				
18	CHARGES			
19	EXERCISE 17			

Notes:

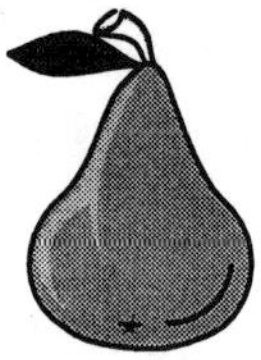

Exercise 18 - Entering Values, Aligning Labels, Resaving

RESAVE AS: FRUIT

John has added fruit that is in season to his fresh fruit stand. He also would like to enter into the spreadsheet the values for amount sold and cost per unit.

Directions

1. Retrieve FRUIT.
2. Widen column A to 12 spaces.
3. Center all labels in columns A and B.
4. Also center the column headings in C4, C5, D4 and D5.
5. Enter the new information in rows 13, 14, 15 and 16. Remember the .2 is actually .20 cents but the zero will drop off.
6. Adjust exercise number.
7. RESAVE AS: FRUIT.

	A	B	C	D
1		JOHN'S FRESH FRUIT		
2		WEEK ENDING JULY 16, 1995		
3				
4			AMOUNT	COST
5	PRODUCT	UNITS	SOLD	PER UNIT
6				
7	BANANAS	POUND	17	0.2
8	PLUMS	POUND	26	0.19
9	PEACHES	POUND	29	0.12
10	CHERRIES	PINT	19	0.33
11	PEARS	POUND	9	0.22
12	KIWI	EACH	17	0.2
13	GRAPEFRUIT	EACH	23	0.14
14	HONEYDEW	EACH	13	0.44
15	CANTELOUPE	EACH	19	0.3
16	NECTARINES	POUND	19	0.28
17				
18				
19				
20				
21	FRUIT			
22	EXERCISE 18			

Notes:

Exercise 19 - Entering Labels and Values, Column Widths, Saving, Naming

SAVE AS: INCOME

The president of Lacy's Department store would like to analyze the net income or loss for one year. Later, she may decide to analyze the net income or loss from several past years.

HELPFUL HINTS

- ➔ Be careful when spacing this income statement. The subcategorizes (GROSS SALES, RETURNS, ETC) are indented two spaces each.
- ➔ This is actually an accounting statement used to show total NET INCOME or LOSS.
- ➔ Negatives do appear in business spreadsheets. They are quite common in the corporate environment.
- ➔ The top part of the spreadsheet will scroll off the screen as you enter the bottom part of the spreadsheet.
- ➔ Check for accuracy. A mistyped number could cost your company money.
- ➔ When typing values in the thousands, do not type the comma.
- ➔ Be careful when entering the information in B4.

Directions:

1. Enter the spreadsheet exactly as shown. When typing information in cells A6 and A7 and all other indented cells, space twice before typing the data.
2. Widen column A to 34 spaces.
3. You will add formulas to this spreadsheet later.
4. SAVE AS: INCOME.

	A	B	C
1	LACY'S INCOME STATEMENT		
2			
3			
4	SALES	1ST YEAR	
5			
6	GROSS SALES	79665	
7	RETURNS	1754	
8	NET SALES		
9			
10			
11	COST OF GOODS SOLD		
12			
13	PURCHASE PRICE	39844	
14	FREIGHT	2002	
15	TOTAL COST OF GOODS SOLD		
16			
17	GROSS PROFIT		
18			
19			
20	OPERATING COSTS		
21			
22	INTEREST	19000	
23	ADMINISTRATIVE	4052	
24	DEPRECIATION	2054	
25	TOTAL OPERATING COSTS		
26			
27			
28	OPERATING INCOME BEFORE TAXES		
29	TAXES	3998	
30			
31	NET INCOME/LOSS		
32			
33	INCOME		
34	EXERCISE 19		

Exercise 20 - Retrieving, Editing with Typeover and the Edit Key, Printing

RESAVE AS: LUIGI

Luigi has decided to add a few more items to his original redecoration list. He also would like to edit a few of his item selections. Be careful to resave and replace after all the changes have been made.

HELPFUL HINTS

- ➔ Try editing by typing the new information or by using the Edit key.
- ➔ Follow directions in order.
- ➔ When resaving and replacing a file, the original file is overridden by the new file.

Directions

1. Retrieve LUIGI.
2. Erase A26 and A27.
3. Widen column A to 30 spaces.
4. Use the edit command to add the word SERVING in front of the word PLATTERS in cell A7.
5. In A23, change CANDLEABRAS to CANDLES FOR TABLES.
6. Change the value in B23 from 45.55 to 17.25.
7. Change the value in C23 from 25 to 27.
8. Add the new labels and values as shown and skip a row between each new item.
9. Erase cells A1 and A2 and retype the heading in B1 and B2.
10. Retype the file name and exercise number.
11. RESAVE AS: LUIGI.
12. Print the spreadsheet.

	A	B	C	D
1		LUIGI'S HOMEMADE PASTA PALACE		
2		NEW REMODELING INVENTORY		
3				
4		COST PER	NUMBER OF	
5	ITEM	ITEM	ITEMS	
6				
7	SERVING PLATTERS	22.55	45	
8				
9	NAPKINS	2.35	100	
10				
11	CREAMERS	5.67	50	
12				
13	PLACEMATS	5.75	50	
14				
15	SUGAR BOWLS	5.67	15	
16				
17	TABLECLOTHS	9.5	35	
18				
19	TABLE PADS	11	30	
20				
21	SALAD BOWLS	4.56	15	
22				
23	CANDLES FOR TABLES	17.25	27	
24				
25	SALT SHAKERS	3.25	50	
26				
27	PEPPER SHAKERS	3.25	50	
28				
29	CHEESE SHAKERS	3.95	50	
30				
31	SILVERWARE (SERVICE 12)	110	14	
32				
33	DISHES (SERVICE 12)	97	14	
34				
35	SERVING SPOONS (SILVER)	12.56	40	
36				
37	SERVING FORKS (SILVER)	11.35	40	
38				
39	NAPKIN RINGS	2.95	100	
40				
41	ICE BUCKETS	7.65	30	
42				
43	HANGING FLOWERS	55.65	12	
44				
45	LUIGI			
46	EXERCISE 20			

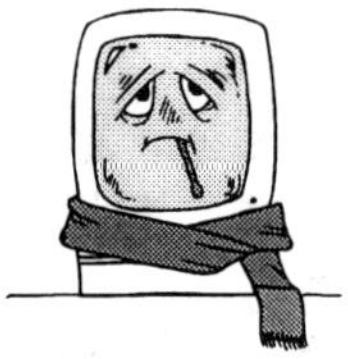

Exercise 21 - Concepts Summary Exercise

SAVE AS: HEALED

I. M. Healed Drug Emporium would like an inventory report for the month ending May, 1996.

HELPFUL HINTS

➔ Create a spreadsheet heading in rows 1 and 2.
➔ Widen and narrow columns where necessary.
➔ Center all column headings.
➔ Check for accuracy and edit all errors.

Directions

1. Write the following information on the grid and then enter it into the computer.

ITEM	UNIT	DESIRED STOCK	PRESENT STOCK
BAND AIDS	BOXED	200	90
ASPIRIN	BOTTLES	1000	50
TOOTHPASTE	TUBES	250	150
LIGHT BULBS	PACKAGE	80	50
HEATING PADS	BOXED	23	20
GAUZE	BOXED	150	50
THERMOMETERS	BOXED	80	23
ALCOHOL	BOTTLES	300	155
FOOT SPRAY	CANS	45	30
LEG BANDAGES	BOXED	28	9
EYE DROPS	BOXED	97	80
BABY FORMULA	CANS	375	62

2. Type the name of the spreadsheet (HEALED) and EXERCISE 21 on the model.
3. SAVE AS: HEALED.

	A	B	C	D	E	F	G	H
1								
2								
3								
4								
5								
6								
7								
8								
9								
10								
11								
12								
13								
14								
15								
16								
17								
18								
19								
20								
21								
22								
23								
24								
25								
26								
27								

Exercise 22 - Concepts Summary Exercise

SAVE AS: PHONE

Maria is a college student and shares an apartment with two other roommates. With three students making several long distance calls, they decided to keep a record of all calls and their approximate time in minutes each month. This makes it much easier when the phone bill arrives.

HELPFUL HINTS

- Create a spreadsheet heading in rows 1 and 2.
- Widen and narrow columns where necessary.
- Center all column headings.
- You may not be able to view this entire spreadsheet on one screen.

Directions

1. Use the following information to write the spreadsheet on the grid on the next page.

STUDENT	DATE	TIME	TYPE	PLACE	NUMBER	MIN	COST PER MIN
MARIA	2/2/95	8:25	NGHT	MEDIA, PA	610-566-9898	6	0.87
ELYSE	2/2/95	9:05	NGHT	DENVER,CO	303-521-9876	4	1.12
MARIA	2/5/95	2:10	DAY	MEDIA, PA	610-566-9898	7	1.2
MISSY	2/8/95	5:50	WKED	DOVER,DE	302-285-1224	2	0.64
MARIA	2/13/95	9:50	WKED	MEDIA, PA	610-566-9898	12	0.77
ELYSE	2/23/95	1:50	DAY	DENVER,CO	303-521-9876	7	1.65

2. Enter the spreadsheet into the computer.
3. Most columns will need an adjustment in column widths.
4. Center all column headings, dates, times, and phone numbers.
5. SAVE AS: PHONE.

	A	B	C	D	E	F	G	H
1								
2								
3								
4								
5								
6								
7								
8								
9								
10								
11								
12								
13								
14								
15								
16								
17								
18								
19								
20								
21								
22								
23								
24								
25								
26								
27								

Competencies

After completing this unit, you will know how to:

1. Resave a file
2. Retrieve a file
3. Align labels—left, right, and center
4. Change column widths
5. Erase cells
6. Edit with the edit key

UNIT 4

Concepts:

Writing and Entering Formulas
Prioritizing Formulas with Parentheses
Percentages in Formulas
Changing Column Widths
Printing

Points to Remember:

- ➲ ***IMPORTANT**: All shaded areas on the spreadsheets in your book are for your use to write formulas for later reference. Write the formulas in your book and then enter them into the computer.*
- ➲ Only the calculated answer appears in the cell with a formula. The formula itself appears on the formula bar, or upper left corner of the screen.
- ➲ Operators are symbols used by the program to calculate values. Do not use any blank spaces when typing in formulas.
- ➲ Use cell addresses to develop formulas–*not the values themselves*. Any change to those values in the cells will automatically change the calculated answer.
- ➲ You can enter formulas by typing or pointing (highlighting). Be particularly careful with subtraction formulas. Place a (-) in front of the cell to be subtracted. Example: to subtract G2 from G3, your answer would be G3-G2. You are subtracting G2 *from* G3 so start with G3.
- ➲ Use parentheses to control the order of operation.
- ➲ When using percentages in a formula, simply type the value as a percent with the percent sign, and the software will change it to a decimal for you. Example: to enter the formula, cell D7 times 7 and one–half percent. Simply type D7*7.5 % and press Enter. The software will change the formula to D7*.075 automatically. Look at the formula bar, or upper left of your screen to see it change.

Exercise 23 - Vertical and Horizontal Formulas, Resaving

RESAVE AS: BASEBALL

The baseball manager needs to compute a total amount of shirts, pants, hats, and gloves for all of the teams.

HELPFUL HINTS

- ➔ All shaded areas in the book are to write formulas for later reference.
- ➔ The formula does not appear in the cell; only the calculated answer appears. It appears in the upper left of the screen.
- ➔ Operators are symbols used by the program to calculate values.
- ➔ Start the formula with the correct operator.
- ➔ The calculated value will right align in the cell.

Directions

1. Retrieve BASEBALL.
2. Write the formulas in your book for TOTAL shirts in B18, pants in C18, hats in D18 and gloves in cell E18.
3. Adjust the exercise number.
4. Type the word TOTAL in cell A18.
5. Enter the formulas into the computer.
6. RESAVE AS: BASEBALL.

	A	B	C	D	E
1	LITTLE LEAGUE INVENTORY				
2	MAY, 1995				
3					
4	TEAM	SHIRTS	PANTS	HATS	GLOVES
5					
6	BLUE JAYS	23	21	23	9
7					
8	CARDINALS	25	25	26	9
9					
10	HAWKS	22	23	24	10
11					
12	EAGLES	21	21	22	9
13					
14	FALCONS	27	26	25	10
15					
16	RAVENS	27	26	25	11
17					
18	TOTAL				
19					
20	BASEBALL				
21	EXERCISE 23				

Notes:

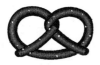

Exercise 24 - Horizontal and Vertical Formulas, Resaving

RESAVE AS: VENDOR

Vinnie would like total sales for each month and total sales for each item in the first quarter.

HELPFUL HINTS

- ➔ Blank spaces should not be included in a formula.
- ➔ Use the cell addresses in these formulas – not the values. For example: B6+B8+B19 *not 212+290+320.*
- ➔ If the cell with the formula reads ERR or zeros instead of the calculated answer, check your values as well as the formula.

Directions

1. Retrieve VENDOR.
2. In your book, write the formulas in all the shaded areas to compute the TOTAL for January in H6, February in H8, and March in H10.
3. In your book, write the formulas in the shaded area to compute the TOTAL for each item (in cells B12, C12, D12, E12, F12, and G12) for the quarter. You do not need a formula in H12.
4. Enter all formulas into the computer.
5. Type the word TOTAL in A12 and H4, and center it.
6. Adjust the exercise number.
7. RESAVE AS: VENDOR.

	A	B	C	D	E	F	G	H
1								
2		FRESH DAILY VENDORS -- FIRST QUARTER						
3								
4		HOT DOGS	PIZZA	PRETZELS	SANDWICHES	HAMBURGERS	SALAD	TOTAL
5								
6	JANUARY	212	289	431	303	190	270	
7								
8	FEBRUARY	290	329	449	360	266	340	
9								
10	MARCH	320	354	457	377	321	367	
11								
12	TOTAL							
13								
14	VENDOR							
15	EXERCISE 24							

Notes:

Credit — Exercise 25 - Formulas, Column Widths, Resaving

RESAVE AS: CHARGES

Zak Johnson would now like a current balance for each charge and a total owed on all the charges so he can better plan his spending for next month.

HELPFUL HINTS

- ➔ There should be no negatives in the NEW BALANCE column.
- ➔ Be careful when subtracting.

Directions

1. Retrieve CHARGES.
2. In E7 write the formula in your book that would show the NEW BALANCE (how much you still owe ZISA).
3. Write the formulas in your book that show the NEW BALANCE for cells E8 through E15.
4. Continue to write the formula in your book in C17 that shows his TOTAL balance on all of Zak's charges.
5. Write a formula in D17 to show TOTAL of payments and in E17 the TOTAL of NEW BALANCE.
6. Change column D to 11 spaces wide.
7. Type the word TOTAL in A17.
8. Type NEW BALANCE in E5 and widen to 15 spaces.
9. Enter all formulas into the computer.
10. Adjust the exercise number.
11. RESAVE AS: CHARGES.

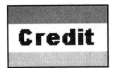

	A	B	C	D	E
1					
2	ZAK'S CHARGES				
3	FIRST QUARTER				
4					
5	CHARGE	ACCOUNT NO.	BALANCE	PAYMENT	NEW BALANCE
6					
7	ZISA	12-99-9821	309	120	
8	J.S.GOODS	45-90-8788	187	60	
9	COSMO	65-87-2332	97	45	
10	LACY	76-98-9899	24	24	
11	ALBERTO	23-23-2322	65	65	
12	THE RAP	11-32-2997	15	15	
13	COLEMAN	33-98-3433	120	30	
14	DRY GOODS	24-87-8789	54	30	
15	PENS,ETC.	99-76-9898	80	80	
16					
17	TOTAL				
18	CHARGES				
19	EXERCISE 25				

Notes:

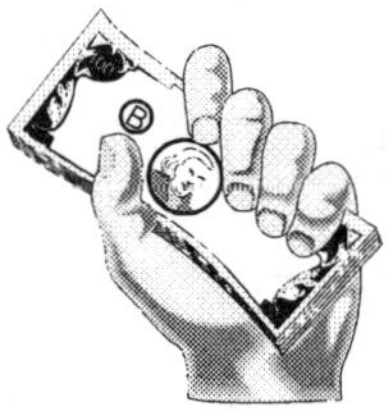

Exercise 26 - Formulas, Aligning Labels, Column Widths, Saving

SAVE AS: SALARY

The following spreadsheet is a salary report for the week ending May 30, 1995. Always proofread for accuracy.

HELPFUL HINTS

- ➔ Be careful when entering information into columns B and C.
- ➔ Center columns B and C as a range.
- ➔ Multiplication and division formulas may result in a calculated answer with varied decimal places. These answers can be rounded later.

Directions

1. Enter the spreadsheet exactly as shown.
2. Change the column width as follows:

    Column A -- 20
    Column B -- 18
    Column C -- 10
    Column D -- 8
    Column E -- 10
    Column F -- 10

3. Center column headings.
4. Center the contents of columns B and C.

5. Write the formula in your book to compute GROSS PAY for James Thompson in cell F7.
6. Write the formulas to compute GROSS PAY for each employee in F8 through F13.
7. Enter all formulas into the computer.
8. SAVE AS: SALARY.

	A	B	C	D	E	F
1	SALARY REPORT					
2	WEEK ENDING MAY 30, 1995					
3						
4		SOCIAL SECURITY	DATE	TOTAL	HOURLY	GROSS
5	NAME	NUMBER	HIRED	HOURS	RATE	PAY
6						
7	THOMPSON, JAMES	123-78-9087	1/14/89	40	9.25	
8	FASSETT, RICHARD	989-87-8876	9/7/75	50	14.55	
9	HIBBERD, BETSY	665-65-7654	6/5/88	35	12.65	
10	COLEMAN, TRACY	565-88-1212	12/12/94	40	7.95	
11	ROYCHOUD, ALBERT	342-76-9981	5/17/69	47	22.67	
12	ALYANAKIAN, LOUIS	357-63-0070	12/19/83	32	11.55	
13	WHEAT, CINDERELLA	769-31-5432	4/29/80	40	13.95	
14						
15						
16						
17	SALARY					
18	EXERCISE 26					

Notes:

Exercise 27 - Aligning Labels, Formulas, Resaving, Printing

RESAVE AS: LUIGI

Luigi is now ready to compute Total Cost of the items he needs for his remodeling at Luigi's Homemade Pasta Palace.

HELPFUL HINTS

- ➔ In the calculated answer, the decimal places may round differently in each cell; some will round to a whole number while other calculated answers will have a varied number of decimal places in the TOTAL COST column.
- ➔ Be careful to use the correct operators.
- ➔ This is a large spreadsheet and may print on two pages.
- ➔ Check your values for accuracy and look at your screen as you enter the formulas.

Directions

1. Retrieve LUIGI.
2. Write the formula in your book in cell D7 to compute TOTAL COST for SERVING PLATTERS.
3. Continue writing formulas in column D to compute TOTAL COST for *each* ITEM.
4. In cell D4, type TOTAL and in cell D5, type COST.
5. Center align D4 and D5.
6. Enter all formulas into the computer.
7. Adjust the exercise number.
8. RESAVE AS: LUIGI.
9. Print.

	A	B	C	D
1		LUIGI'S HOMEMADE PASTA PALACE		
2		NEW REMODELING INVENTORY		
3				
4		COST PER	NUMBER OF	TOTAL
5	ITEM	ITEM	ITEMS	COST
6				
7	SERVING PLATTERS	22.55	45	
8				
9	NAPKINS	2.35	100	
10				
11	CREAMERS	5.67	50	
12				
13	PLACEMATS	5.75	50	
14				
15	SUGAR BOWLS	5.67	15	
16				
17	TABLECLOTHS	9.5	35	
18				
19	TABLE PADS	11	30	
20				
21	SALAD BOWLS	4.56	15	
22				
23	CANDLES FOR TABLES	17.25	27	
24				
25	SALT SHAKERS	3.25	50	
26				
27	PEPPER SHAKERS	3.25	50	
28				
29	CHEESE SHAKERS	3.95	50	
30				
31	SILVERWARE (SERVICE 12)	110	14	
32				
33	DISHES (SERVICE 12)	97	14	
34				
35	SERVING SPOONS (SILVER)	12.56	40	
36				
37	SERVING FORKS (SILVER)	11.35	40	
38				
39	NAPKIN RINGS	2.95	100	
40				
41	ICE BUCKETS	7.65	30	
42				
43	HANGING FLOWERS	55.65	12	
44				
45	EXERCISE 27			
46	LUIGI			

Exercise 28 - Formulas, and Resaving

RESAVE AS: CARS

Bill Thompson would like the total number of cars each salesperson sold for the first quarter of the year.

HELPFUL HINTS

➔ Put the formula in the cell where you want the calculated answer.
➔ The symbols used in formulas are called operators.
➔ When you use cell addresses to create formulas, you are building a template so that any change to the value will cause the answer to recalculate automatically.

Directions

1. Retrieve CARS.
2. Write the formula in your book in cell E8 to find TOTAL sales for salesperson Pilio for the first quarter.
3. Write the remaining formulas in your book for cells E9 through E19.
4. Type the word TOTAL in cell E6.
5. Enter the formulas in the computer.
6. RESAVE AS: CARS.

	A	B	C	D	E
1	BILL'S A-1 USED CARS				
2	SALESPEOPLE REPORT				
3	FIRST QUARTER				
4	TOTAL CARS SOLD				
5					
6	SALESREP	JANUARY	FEBRUARY	MARCH	TOTAL
7					
8	PILIO	12	15	9	
9	COCHRAN	5	9	15	
10	GUNKLE	18	19	18	
11	BELL	11	12	10	
12	LOMBARDO	22	19	20	
13	ULLMAN	13	14	12	
14	SULLIVAN	21	24	23	
15	SHADE	15	15	5	
16	WESTON	19	18	17	
17	ASSOUSA	15	16	16	
18	KLOPP	17	22	27	
19	PARKER	15	17	19	
20					
21					
22	CARS				
23	EXERCISE 28				

Notes:

Exercise 29 - Formulas, Aligning Cells, Resaving

RESAVE AS: FRUIT

John would like to compute a Total Cost for each item in his fruit stand.

Directions

1. Retrieve FRUIT.
2. Write the formula in your book to compute TOTAL COST for bananas in E7.
3. Continue writing the formulas to compute TOTAL COST for each kind of fruit in cells E8 to E16.
4. Type TOTAL in E4 and COST in E5 and center them.
5. Using the Edit key, make kiwi in cell A12, grapefruit in A13, and cantaloupe in A15 plural.
6. Enter the formulas into the computer.
7. Adjust the exercise number.
8. RESAVE AS: FRUIT.

	A	B	C	D	E
1		JOHN'S FRESH FRUIT			
2		WEEK ENDING JULY 16,1995			
3					
4			AMOUNT	COST	TOTAL
5	PRODUCT	UNITS	SOLD	PER UNIT	COST
6					
7	BANANAS	POUND	17	0.2	
8	PLUMS	POUND	26	0.19	
9	PEACHES	POUND	29	0.12	
10	CHERRIES	PINT	19	0.33	
11	PEARS	POUND	9	0.22	
12	KIWI	EACH	17	0.2	
13	GRAPEFRUIT	EACH	23	0.14	
14	HONEYDEW	EACH	13	0.44	
15	CANTALOUPE	EACH	19	0.3	
16	NECTARINES	POUND	19	0.28	
17					
18					
19					
20					
21	FRUIT				
22	EXERCISE 29				

Notes:

Exercise 30 - Prioritizing Formulas with Parentheses, Resaving

RESAVE AS: GRADES

Krista's semester is over and she can now get an average for each class.

HELPFUL HINTS

➔ It is important to consider the order of operation in these formulas. All formulas in this exercise must use parentheses.
➔ Your decimals may round differently.
➔ Parentheses control the order of operation regardless of the order set by the spreadsheet application.

Directions

1. Retrieve GRADES.
2. Write the formula in your book to compute the AVERAGE numeric grade in cell F6.
3. Continue writing the formulas in column F to compute the test Average for each course.
4. Type AVERAGE in cell F4.
5. Change the column width of A to 13 spaces.
6. Enter all formulas into the computer.
7. Adjust the exercise number.
8. RESAVE AS: GRADES.

	A	B	C	D	E	F
1	FIRST SEMESTER GRADES					
2	JUNIOR YEAR -- 1995					
3						
4	COURSE	TEST 1	TEST 2	TEST 3	TEST 4	AVERAGE
5						
6	ENGLISH	98	100	91	88	
7						
8	HISTORY	92	90	87	86	
9						
10	SPANISH	97	85	89	90	
11						
12	PHYSICS	99	98	100	100	
13						
14	CALCULUS	100	90	95	91	
15						
16	BIOLOGY	85	87	100	100	
17						
18						
19	GRADES					
20	EXERCISE 30					

Notes:

Exercise 31 - Formulas, Aligning Cells, Column Widths, Resaving

RESAVE AS: CARS

Bill had a good quarter at his used car dealership but he would like a Monthly Total for each month in the first quarter.

Directions

1. Retrieve CARS.
2. Write the formula in your book to compute the MONTHLY TOTALS for January in B21.
3. Continue to write the formulas in columns C, D, and E.
4. Type MONTHLY TOTALS in cell A21.
5. Change column A to a width of 17 and center all column headings.
6. Enter all the formulas into the computer.
7. RESAVE AS: CARS.

	A	B	C	D	E
1	BILL'S A-1 USED CARS				
2	SALESPEOPLE REPORT				
3	FIRST QUARTER				
4	TOTAL CARS SOLD				
5					
6	SALESREP	JANUARY	FEBRUARY	MARCH	TOTAL
7					
8	PILIO	12	15	9	36
9	COCHRAN	5	9	15	29
10	GUNKLE	18	19	18	55
11	BELL	11	12	10	33
12	LOMBARDO	22	19	20	61
13	ULLMAN	13	14	12	39
14	SULLIVAN	21	24	23	68
15	SHADE	15	15	5	35
16	WESTON	19	18	17	54
17	ASSOUSA	15	16	16	47
18	KLOPP	17	22	27	66
19	PARKER	15	17	19	51
20					
21	MONTHLY TOTALS				
22	CARS				
23	EXERCISE 31				

Notes:

Exercise 32 - Formulas, Resaving, Printing

RESAVE AS: INCOME

The Manager of Lacy's department store would like to see the Total Profit or Loss for the year.

HELPFUL HINTS

- ➔ Follow the directions in order.
- ➔ Check each cell address as you enter formulas.
- ➔ Be careful to use the correct operators—especially subtraction.
- ➔ *Only* enter formulas in the *shaded* cells.

Directions

1. Retrieve INCOME.
2. Be aware that SALES in A4, COST OF GOODS SOLD in A11, and OPERATING COSTS in A20 are only headings. NO formulas go in cells B4, B11 or B20.
3. In cell B8, write the formula for NET SALES.
4. In cell B15, write the formula for TOTAL COST OF GOODS SOLD.
5. In cell B17, write the formula to compute GROSS PROFIT. (Subtract the TOTAL COST OF GOODS SOLD from NET SALES.)
6. In cell B25, write the formula for TOTAL OPERATING COSTS.
7. In cell B28, write the formula for OPERATING INCOME BEFORE TAXES. (Subtract the TOTAL OPERATING COSTS from GROSS PROFIT.)
8. In cell B31, write the formula for NET INCOME/LOSS for the year. (Subtract TAXES from OPERATING INCOME BEFORE TAXES.)
9. Enter all formulas into the computer.
10. Adjust the exercise number.
11. RESAVE AS: INCOME and print.

	A	B
1	LACY'S INCOME STATEMENT -- FIRST QUARTER	
2		
3		
4	SALES	1ST YEAR
5		
6	GROSS SALES	79665
7	RETURNS	1754
8	NET SALES	
9		
10		
11	COST OF GOODS SOLD	
12		
13	PURCHASE PRICE	39844
14	FREIGHT	2002
15	TOTAL COST OF GOODS SOLD	
16		
17	GROSS PROFIT	
18		
19		
20	OPERATING COSTS	
21		
22	INTEREST	19000
23	ADMINISTRATIVE	4052
24	DEPRECIATION	2054
25	TOTAL OPERATING COSTS	
26		
27		
28	OPERATING INCOME BEFORE TAXES	
29	TAXES	3998
30		
31	NET INCOME/LOSS	
32		
33	INCOME	
34	EXERCISE 32	

Exercise 33 - Percentages in Formulas, Printing

SAVE AS: MUSIC

Mark and Stephanie are pricing a total entertainment center for their family room. The stereo system would be discounted if *all* parts of the entertainment center were bought together. They would like the Sale Price of each item after the Discount is deducted.

HELPFUL HINTS

➔ When typing a percent, simply type the value as a percent and the software will change it to a decimal for you. For example, type in 5% and the program will automatically change the 5% to .05 in the formula.

➔ The 25% will *only* be in the formula. You will not see it on the screen.

Directions

1. Enter the spreadsheet exactly as shown.
2. The DISCOUNT for each item is 25%. In cell C7, write in your book the formula to compute the DISCOUNT for the 32 inch television. (The 25% will only be in the formula. You will not see it on the screen.)
3. Continue writing the formulas in the computer for the DISCOUNT in cells C8 through C13.
4. In cell D7, write the formula for SALE PRICE for the television. Continue writing the formulas from D8 to D13.
5. Adjust column widths as necessary and center column headings.
6. Enter all formulas into the computer.
7. SAVE AS: MUSIC.
8. Print.

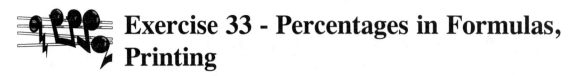

	A	B	C	D
1	21ST CENTURY APPLIANCES			
2	ENTERTAINMENT CENTER			
3				
4		LIST		SALE
5	PRODUCT	PRICE	DISCOUNT	PRICE
6				
7	TELEVISION--32 INCH	999		
8	PROGRAMMABLE VCR	420		
9	RECEIVER	877		
10	AMPLIFIER	665		
11	SPEAKERS	975		
12	TAPE DECK	355		
13	CD PLAYER	395		
14				
15				
16	MUSIC			
17	EXERCISE 33			

Notes:

Exercise 34 - Formulas, Formulas with Parentheses, Printing

SAVE AS: DOCTOR

Your employer, Dr. Anna Stesia, would like to keep a record of her patients' names, ages, and dates examined. She would also like a record of amount due, amount paid and amount owed by each patient for the week ending October 17, 1994.

Directions

1. Enter the spreadsheet as shown.
2. Write the formulas on the grid in column F in the shaded cells in the book to show AMOUNT OWED by each patient.
3. Write a formula for cell F16 to find AVERAGE AMOUNT OWED and enter it into the computer.
4. Center all column headings and dates.
5. Enter the formulas into the computer.
6. SAVE AS: DOCTOR
7. Print.

	A	B	C	D	E	F
1			DR. ANNA STESIA			
2			PATIENT REPORT			
3			WEEK ENDING OCTOBER 17, 1994			
4						
5	PATIENT	AGE	DATE EXAMINED	DUE	PAID	AMOUNT OWED
6						
7	O'SULLIVAN, AMY	24	10/11/94	127	127	
8	ROTHERFORD, MARY	56	10/11/94	78	50	
9	HIGGINS, JAMES	43	10/13/94	219	0	
10	BROTHERSTON, FRED	77	10/13/94	45	45	
11	MEDINA, JOSE	42	10/14/94	45	20	
12	CALLAGHAN, SUSAN	37	10/15/94	90	70	
13	CELLINI, ANTHONY	64	10/15/94	137	27	
14						
15						
16	AVERAGE					
17						
18	DOCTOR					
19	EXERCISE 34					

Notes:

Exercise 35 - Concepts Summary Exercise

SAVE AS: BLUE

Records will be kept for Betty Sky's Blueberry Farm. Create a model for the Week Ending June 12, 1996. They need the total pounds of blueberries sold per week, total selling price, total amount earned from each company (this is based on pounds sold and selling price) and grand total (their earnings from each company) for the week.

Directions

1. Create the following spreadsheet on the blank grid provided.

COMPANY	PRODUCT	POUNDS SOLD	SELLING PRICE
TASTYFINE	PIES	1200	.56
DUKESBERRY	MUFFINS	900	.57
AUNT JENNY'S	PANCAKES	800	.57
MAMA MARY'S	PIES	450	.57
FRED'S DINER	FRESH	150	.64
MCDOWELL'S	PIES	3500	.50
REGENCY	WAFFLES	350	.57
BERRIES, INC.	COBBLER	425	.57

2. Write the formulas on the grid to compute the following:
   TOTAL earned from each company.
   TOTAL pounds of blueberries sold.
   TOTAL selling price.
   AVERAGE selling price.
   AVERAGE pounds sold.
   GRAND TOTAL earned from all companies.
3. Enter the formulas into the computer.
4. Enter the filename and exercise number on the spreadsheet.
5. SAVE AS: BLUE.
6. Print the spreadsheet.

	A	B	C	D	E	F	G	H
1								
2								
3								
4								
5								
6								
7								
8								
9								
10								
11								
12								
13								
14								
15								
16								
17								
18								
19								
20								
21								
22								
23								
24								
25								
26								
27								

Exercise 36 - Concepts Summary Exercise

SAVE AS: COLLEGE

American University is gathering data for its Population Report for the Fall Semester of 1996. There are eight possible majors at the university. The university needs to keep specific statistics for all males and females who have enrolled, dropped, and who remain in each major.

Directions

1. Create a spreadsheet on the grid.

MAJOR	TOTAL MALES ENROLLED	TOTAL MALES DROPPED	TOTAL FEMALES ENROLLED	TOTAL FEMALES DROPPED
ENGINEERING	780	202	654	121
BUSINESS	1200	198	1187	187
LIBERAL ARTS	1800	331	2020	219
MATH	670	101	865	137
COMPUTER SCIENCE	976	243	895	209
PRE MED	1090	477	760	203
COMMUNICATIONS	1100	132	1150	112
BIOLOGY	943	234	1010	221

2. Enter a formula to show the following statistics:

   TOTAL MALES ENROLLED, DROPPED, AND REMAINING IN EACH MAJOR
   TOTAL FEMALES ENROLLED, DROPPED AND REMAINING IN EACH MAJOR
   GRAND TOTAL REMAINING IN ALL MAJORS

3. Center columns headings and widen or narrow as necessary.
4. Put the file name and the exercise number on spreadsheet.
5. SAVE AS: COLLEGE.
6. Print.

	A	B	C	D	E	F	G	H
1								
2								
3								
4								
5								
6								
7								
8								
9								
10								
11								
12								
13								
14								
15								
16								
17								
18								
19								
20								
21								
22								
23								
24								
25								
26								
27								

Competencies:

After completing this unit, you will know how to:

1. Write horizontal and vertical formulas
2. Enter formulas into the computer
3. Prioritize formulas (control the order of operation) with parentheses
4. Use cell addresses in formulas
5. Use percentages in formulas
6. Type or point formulas
7. Print

UNIT 5

Concepts:

Ranges
Functions
Relative and Absolute Formulas
Copying
Pointing

Points to Remember:

- A range is a group of adjacent cells organized in any of the following: an individual cell, a row, a column, or a block. It is usually in the shape of a rectangle.
- Range commands affect only the range you are working on, not the entire spreadsheet.
- An argument can be a range, a formula, or another function and is usually enclosed in parentheses.
- In a range, electronic spreadsheets treat blank cells and cells with zeros differently. Spreadsheets calculate the zero as a value but ignore blank cells.
- A function is a short cut formula.
- Functions use a structure you must follow. Use a prefix (= or @) followed by a function name (usually a contraction of the full name) and an argument. Example: @SUM(A1..A100) or =SUM(A1:A100).
- Write one of each (sample) formula or functions instead of filling in *all* the formulas or functions in the gray area in your book.
- Copying is a two-step process: where to copy *FROM* and where to copy *TO*.
- Labels or values copy exactly.
- When copying a formula, the formula changes and adapts to its new location. This is called a *relative formula*.
- If you do not want the cell address to adapt when copying, use an *absolute* formula. To make a cell absolute, use a dollar sign *before* the column letter and *before* the row number. Example: A4.

Exercise 37 - Erasing, Functions, Resaving, Printing

RESAVE AS: BASEBALL

The formulas in this model will be erased and all changed to functions.

> **HELPFUL HINTS**
>
> ➔ Functions can be entered by highlighting or typing a range.
> ➔ When erasing a single cell or a range of cells, always look at the screen to check your cell pointer.

Directions

1. Retrieve BASEBALL.
2. Erase the range B18..E18.
3. Enter a function in B18 to add all the shirts needed for all teams.
4. Also enter the function in cells C18, D18 and E18.
5. Type and center the word TOTAL in F4.
6. Enter a function in F6 to add all of the items needed for the Blue Jays.
7. Also enter the functions in cells F8, F10, F12, F14, F16, and F18.
8. Adjust the exercise number.
9. RESAVE AS: BASEBALL.
10. Print.

	A	B	C	D	E	F
1	LITTLE LEAGUE INVENTORY					
2	MAY, 1995					
3						
4	TEAM	SHIRTS	PANTS	HATS	GLOVES	TOTAL
5						
6	BLUE JAYS	23	21	23	9	
7						
8	CARDINALS	25	25	26	9	
9						
10	HAWKS	22	23	24	10	
11						
12	EAGLES	21	21	22	9	
13						
14	FALCONS	27	26	25	10	
15						
16	RAVENS	27	26	25	11	
17						
18	TOTAL					
19						
20	BASEBALL					
21	EXERCISE 37					

Notes:

Exercise 38 - Functions, Copying, Printing

RESAVE AS: CARS

Bill would like a little more information about the sales of his present sales staff. He needs a monthly total, average, and lowest and highest sales for each member of his sales staff.

HELPFUL HINTS

- ➔ From this point on in your exercise book, formulas that are copied can be represented by an arrow instead of writing cach formula.
- ➔ Remember copying is a two step process: where to copy *FROM* and where to copy *TO*. Look at the screen as you copy.

Directions

1. Retrieve CARS.
2. Erase CARS and EXERCISE 28 in cells A22 and A23.
3. Erase range E8..E19 and erase the range A21..E21.
4. Enter a function in E8 to show totals.
5. Copy the function from E8 to E9 through E19.
6. Type the word TOTAL in cell A21, AVERAGE in cell A22, MINIMUM in A23, and MAXIMUM in A24.
7. Write and enter a function in B21 to show TOTAL cars sold for the month of January.
8. Copy the formula from B21 to C21..E21.
9. Write and enter a function in B22 to show AVERAGE cars sold for the month of January.
10. Copy the formula from B22 to C22..E22.
11. Write and enter a function in B23 to show MINIMUM (lowest) amount of cars sold for January.
12. Copy the formula from B23 to C23..E23.
13. Write and enter a function in B24 to show MAXIMUM (highest) amount of cars sold for January.
14. Copy the formula from B24 to C24..E24.
15. Adjust the exercise number and file name and RESAVE AS: CARS. Print.

	A	B	C	D	E
1	BILL'S A-1 USED CARS				
2	SALESPEOPLE REPORT				
3	FIRST QUARTER				
4	TOTAL CARS SOLD				
5					
6	SALESREP	JANUARY	FEBRUARY	MARCH	TOTALS
7					
8	PILIO	12	15	9	
9	COCHRAN	5	9	15	
10	GUNKLE	18	19	18	
11	BELL	11	12	10	
12	LOMBARDO	22	19	20	
13	ULLMAN	13	14	12	
14	SULLIVAN	21	24	23	
15	SHADE	15	15	5	
16	WESTON	19	18	17	
17	ASSOUSA	15	16	16	
18	KLOPP	17	22	27	
19	PARKER	15	17	19	
20					
21	TOTAL				
22	AVERAGE				
23	MINUMUM				
24	MAXIMUM				
25					
26	CARS				
27	EXERCISE 38				

Exercise 39 - Formulas, Functions, Copying, Printing

RESAVE AS: LUIGI

Luigi has decided to compute some of his inventory costs to further plan for his redecoration.

HELPFUL HINTS

- ➔ You can copy functions and formulas. Always check each formula when copying it.
- ➔ You can type or highlight the range when entering formulas and functions.
- ➔ Always check your range.

Directions

1. Retrieve LUIGI.
2. Delete cells A45 and A46.
3. In A45 type TOTAL.
4. In A46 type AVERAGE.
5. In cell B45, enter a function to TOTAL the cost per item from B7..B43.
6. Copy the function from B45 to C45..D45.
7. In B46, enter a function to AVERAGE the cost per item from B7..B43.
8. Copy the function from B46 to C46..D46.
9. Type LUIGI in A48 and EXERCISE 39 in A49.
10. RESAVE AS: LUIGI.
11. Print.

	A	B	C	D
1		LUIGI'S HOMEMADE PASTA PALACE		
2		NEW REMODELING INVENTORY		
3				
4		COST PER	NUMBER OF	TOTAL COST
5	ITEM	ITEM	ITEMS	OF ITEM
6				
7	SERVING PLATTERS	22.55	45	1014.75
8				
9	NAPKINS	2.35	100	235
10				
11	CREAMERS	5.67	50	283.5
12				
13	PLACEMATS	5.75	50	287.5
14				
15	SUGAR BOWLS	5.67	15	85.05
16				
17	TABLECLOTHS	9.5	60	570
18				
19	TABLE PADS	11	30	330
20				
21	SALAD BOWLS	4.56	15	68.4
22				
23	CANDLES FOR TABLES	17.25	27	465.75
24				
25	SALT SHAKERS	3.25	50	162.5
26				
27	PEPPER SHAKERS	3.25	50	162.5
28				
29	CHEESE SHAKERS	3.95	50	197.5
30				
31	SILVERWARE (SERVICE 12)	110	14	1540
32				
33	DISHES (SERVICE 12)	97	14	1358
34				
35	SERVING SPOONS (SILVER)	12.56	40	502.4
36				
37	SERVING FORKS (SILVER)	11.35	40	454
38				
39	NAPKIN RINGS	2.95	100	295
40				
41	ICE BUCKETS	7.65	30	229.5
42				
43	HANGING FLOWERS	55.65	12	667.8
44				
45	TOTAL			
46	AVERAGE			
47				
48	LUIGI			
49	EXERCISE 39			

Exercise 40 - Formulas, Functions, Copying

SAVE AS: COMMISS

Calderi's Real Estate would like to make a commission report for the week ending May 30, 1996. Each salesperson received 6% commission on their total sales. They also make a base salary of $1500.

HELPFUL HINTS

➔ No formula goes in column D, only values.
➔ Notice that values and labels copy exactly while formulas change their cell addresses to adjust to their new location. This is called a relative reference.

Directions

1. Enter the spreadsheet exactly as shown.
2. Enter the commission rate of 6 percent in cell D8. (You may enter it as .06).
3. Copy the contents of cell D8 into cells D9..D15.
4. Enter a formula in E8 to show commission paid to each salesperson.
5. Copy the contents of cell E8 into cells E9..E15.
6. The BASE SALARY for all employees is 1500. Enter that amount in cell F8.
7. Copy the contents of cell F8 into cells F9..F15.
8. Enter a function in G8 to compute TOTAL SALARY.
9. Copy the contents of cell G8 into cells G9..G15.
10. Enter a function in cell E17 to compute TOTAL commission.
11. Copy the contents of E17 into cells F17..G17.
12. SAVE AS: COMMISS.

	A	B	C	D	E	F	G
1	CALDERI'S REAL ESTATE						
2	COMMISSION REPORT						
3	WEEK ENDING MAY 30, 1996						
4							
5				COMM.			TOTAL
6	AGENT	LOCATION	SALES	RATE	COMMISSION	BASE SALARY	SALARY
7							
8	LOCKWOOD	LOGANWOOD	987000				
9	DEADY	THORNBURY	634000				
10	BELSASCO	PINEHURST	854000				
11	SOSTMANN	WILLOUGHBY	550000				
12	POWELL	LOGANWOOD	654000				
13	WHITMORE	PINEHURST	439000				
14	SONG	MONACO	689000				
15	COAKLEY	THORNBURY	320000				
16							
17	TOTAL						
18	COMMISS						
19	EXERCISE 40						

Notes:

Exercise 41 - Formulas, Functions, Copying, Printing

RESAVE AS: MUSIC

Mark and Stephanie also need to compute the Sales Tax (7 percent) on each item and the Total Price with the Sales Tax.

HELPFUL HINTS

➔ The percent will not be visible on the screen in column E. It will be entered in the formula.
➔ Only use functions for TOTAL in row 15.

Directions

1. Retrieve MUSIC.
2. Enter the new labels as shown in cells E4, E5, F4 and F5 and center them.
3. Type TOTAL in A15.
4. In cell E7, enter a formula to compute SALES TAX; the SALES TAX is 7 percent. Hint: this is the amount of sales tax paid by Mark and Stephanie.
5. Copy the formula from E7 to E8..E13.
6. In cell F7, enter a formula to compute TOTAL PRICE of the television.
7. Copy the formula from F7 to F8..F13.
8. Enter a function in B15 to compute TOTAL list price.
9. Copy the formula from B15 to C15..F15.
10. RESAVE AS: MUSIC.
11. Print.

	A	B	C	D	E	F
1	21ST CENTURY APPLIANCE					
2	ENTERTAINMENT CENTER					
3						
4		LIST		SALE	SALES	TOTAL
5	PRODUCT	PRICE	DISCOUNT	PRICE	TAX	PRICE
6						
7	TELEVISION--32 INCH	999	249.75	749.25		
8	PROGRAMMABLE VCR	420	105	315		
9	RECEIVER	877	219.25	657.75		
10	AMPLIFIER	665	166.25	498.75		
11	SPEAKERS	975	243.75	731.25		
12	TAPE DECK	355	88.75	266.25		
13	CD PLAYER	395	98.75	296.25		
14						
15	TOTAL					
16	MUSIC					
17	EXERCISE 41					

Notes:

Exercise 42 - Relative and Absolute Formulas

SAVE AS: WEDDING

Vanessa and Michael are planning their wedding and are getting several estimates on their reception. They want to compare the price of four meal choices. They have not decided if they would like to serve hors d'oerves; therefore, they requested the hors d'oerves prices be separate from the meal price and they will look at the total package with or without the hors d'oerves. After they see the comparisons, they will decide on the meal and the hors d'oerves.

HELPFUL HINTS

- ➔ There are many wide columns in this spreadsheet.
- ➔ Your decimals will round differently. You will change that later.
- ➔ Check cell addresses for accuracy.
- ➔ Remember 42.50 will round to 42.5; 8.00 will round to 8, etc.

Directions

1. Enter the spreadsheet exactly as shown.
2. Center all column headings.
3. Enter formulas that show:

   TOTAL MEAL COST OF ALL GUESTS for each of the four choices for 100 guests at the Mont Chateau Restaurant – *absolute formula.*
   TOTAL COST FOR THE HORS D'OERVES for each of the four choices for 100 guests – a*bsolute formula.*
   TOTAL MEAL AND HORS D'OERVES COST for each of the four choices – *relative formula.*

4. SAVE AS: WEDDING.

	A	B	C	D	E	F
1		MICHAEL AND VANESSA'S WEDDING				
2		RECEPTION ARRANGEMENTS				
3						
4						
5	AMOUNT OF GUESTS			100		
6						
7						
8	MONT CHATEAU RESTAURANT					
9						
10	RECEPTION	MEAL PER	TOTAL MEAL COST	HORS D'OERVES	HORS	MEAL AND
11	MENU	PERSON	OF ALL GUESTS	PER PERSON	D'OERVES	HORS D'OERVES
12						
13	CHICKEN DIANE	42.50		7.50		
14	SIRLOIN TIPS	47.50		8.00		
15	PORK CHOPS	55.00		8.50		
16	SURF AND TURF	66.75		9.50		
17						
18						
19	WEDDING					
20	EXERCISE 42					

Notes:

Exercise 43 - Absolute Formulas, Functions, Copying, Printing

RESAVE AS: EXPENSES

The Sweets Candy Company has had a steady increase in expenses over their first four years. The annual increase rate is 6.25%. Make sure you not only add the percent of the increase but also add the expenses from the previous year.

Directions

1. Retrieve EXPENSES.
2. Enter ANNUAL INCREASE RATE in cell A4.
3. Enter the value 6.25% in cell B4. Depending on your software, you may have to enter it as .0625.
4. Enter the labels YEAR 2 in cell C6, YEAR 3 in D6 and YEAR 4 in E6.
5. Enter an absolute formula in cell C8 to show the increase plus the rent paid from YEAR 1. (Be careful to not only multiply the rent by the percent, but add the rent amount paid from YEAR 1. This is an absolute formula.)
6. Copy the formula from C8 to C9..C13.
7. Copy the formula from C8 to D8.
8. Copy the formula from D8 to D9..D13.
9. Copy the formula from D8 to E8.
10. Copy the formula from E8 to E9..E13.
11. Enter a function in cell B15 to show TOTAL expenses for YEAR 1.
12. Copy the function from B15 to C15..E15.
13. SAVE AS: EXPENSES.
14. Print.

	A	B	C	D	E
1	PROJECTION OF BUSINESS EXPENSES				
2	SWEETS CANDY COMPANY				
3					
4	ANNUAL INCREASE RATE:	6%			
5					
6	EXPENSES	YEAR 1	YEAR 2	YEAR 3	YEAR 4
7					
8	RENT	14567			
9	UTILITIES	1198			
10	MACHINERY UPKEEP	1010			
11	SALARIES	387000			
12	ADVERTISING	8235			
13	DELIVERY/FREIGHT	1500			
14					
15	TOTAL				
16					
17	EXPENSES				
18	EXERCISE 43				

Notes:

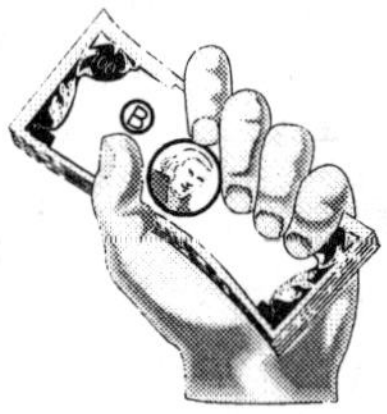

Exercise 44 - Formulas, Functions, Copying

RESAVE AS: SALARY

The salary report for the week ending May 30, 1995 needs to include F.W.T (Federal Withholding Tax) and S.S.T (Social Security Tax). The F.W.T. is 20 percent and the S.S.T. is 7.15 percent.

HELPFUL HINTS

- ➔ Two new employees were hired in May and need to be added to this spreadsheet.
- ➔ The F.W.T. and S.S.T. are deductions from Gross Pay to get the Net Pay.
- ➔ You will not see the percentages on your screen. They will be in the formulas.
- ➔ This may print on two pages.

Directions

1. Retrieve SALARY.
2. Enter the new information in rows 14 and 15.
3. Erase cells A17 and A18.
4. Compute the two new employees' gross pay by copying the formula from F13 to F14 and F15.
5. In cell G5, type F.W.T. In cell H5 type, S.S.T. and in cell I5 type NET PAY.
6. In cell G7 enter the formula to compute F.W.T. (20% x Gross Pay).
7. Copy the formula from G7 into G8..G15.
8. In cell H7 enter the formula to compute S.S.T.
9. Copy the formula from H7 into H8..H15.
10. Enter the formula in I7 to compute NET PAY.
11. Copy the formula from I7 into I8..I15.
12. Type TOTAL in A17, AVERAGE in A18, MINIMUM in A19, and MAXIMUM in A20.

13. In cell D17 enter a function to compute TOTAL hours.
14. Copy the function from D17 into E17..I17.
15. In cell D18 enter a function to compute AVERAGE hours.
16. Copy the function from D18 into E18..I18.
17. In cell D19 enter a function to compute MINIMUM (lowest) hours.
18. Copy the function from D19 into E19..I19.
19. In cell D20 enter a function to compute MAXIMUM (highest) hours.
20. Copy the function from D20 into E20..I20.
21. Enter the file name and exercise number on spreadsheet.
22. RESAVE AS: SALARY.
23. Print.

	A	B	C	D	E	F	G	H	I
1	SALARY REPORT								
2	WEEK ENDING MAY 30, 1995								
3									
4		SOCIAL SECURITY	DATE	TOTAL	HOURLY	GROSS			
5	NAME	NUMBER	HIRED	HOURS	RATE	PAY	F.W.T.	S.S.T.	NET PAY
6									
7	THOMPSON, JAMES	123-78-9087	1/14/82	40	9.25	370			
8	FASSETT, RICHARD	989-87-8876	9/7/75	50	14.55	728			
9	HIBBERD, BETSY	665-65-7654	6/5/88	35	12.65	443			
10	COLEMAN, TRACY	565-88-1212	12/12/94	40	7.95	318			
11	ROYCHOUD, ALBERT	342-76-9981	5/17/69	47	22.67	1065			
12	ALYANAKIAN, LOUIS	357-63-0070	12/19/83	32	11.55	370			
13	WHEAT, CINDERELLA	769-31-5432	4/29/80	40	13.95	558			
14	THOMPSON, CHRIS	231-98-6665	5/23/95	44	7.75				
15	GREY, EVELYN	665-01-0041	5/25/95	36	8.1				
16									
17	TOTAL								
18	AVERAGE								
19	MINIMUM								
20	MAXIMUM								
21									
22	SALARY								
23	EXERCISE 44								
24									

Notes:

Exercise 45 - Absolute Formulas, Copying, "What Ifs," Printing

RESAVE AS: WEDDING

Vanessa and Michael have decided to get estimates from two other restaurants on meal and hors d'oerve prices. They would like to compare the different meal prices, the hors d'oerve prices and the total price from *each* restaurant.

Directions

1. Retrieve WEDDING.
2. The following are copy commands:
   Copy the labels from A10..A16 to A22..A28.
   Copy the labels from B10..F11 to B22..F23.
3. Type WALLINGFORD INN in cell A20.
4. Enter the following information in columns B and for the WALLINGFORD INN: The chicken diane at the Wallingford Inn is $46.75 (hors d'oerves–$6.30); the sirloin tips are $49.00 (hors d'oerves–$7.00); the pork chops are $54.50 (hors d'oerves–$7.50); and the surf–and–turf is $68.75 (hors d'oerves–$8.25).
5. The following are copy commands:
   Copy the formula from C16 to C25..C28.
   Copy the formula from E16 to E25..E28.
   Copy the formula from F16 to F25..F28.
6. Type ROMEO AND JULIET CASTLE INN in cell A32.
7. The following are copy commands.
   Copy the labels from A22..A28 to A34..A40.
   Copy the labels from B22..F23 to B34..F35.
8. Enter the following information in column B for the ROMEO AND JULIET CASTLE INN.
   The chicken diane is $50.50 (hors d'oerves--$7.25); the sirloin tips are $53.60 (hors d'oerves--$7.75); the pork chops are $57.75 (hors d'oerves--$8.65); and the surf–and–turf is $73.50 (hors d'oerves--$9.25).
9. The following are copy commands:
   Copy the formula from C28 to C37..C40.
   Copy the formula from E28 to E37..E40.
   Copy the formula from F28 to F37..F40.
10. Enter the file name and exercise number on the spreadsheet.
11. SAVE AS: WEDDING.
12. Print.

13. "What If" they wanted to invite 150 guests? Change the amount of guests in cell D5 from 100 to 150 and check all the values. Look at your screen and watch most of the values change.
14. Save as WED150 and print.
15. "What If" they wanted to invite 200 guests? Change the amount of guests in cell D5 from 150 to 200 and check all the values. Watch most of the values change.
16. SAVE AS: WED200 and print.

	A	B	C	D	E	F
1		MICHAEL AND VANESSA'S WEDDING				
2		RECEPTION ARRANGEMENTS				
3						
4						
5	AMOUNT OF GUESTS			100		
6						
7	MONT CHATEAU RESTAURANT					
8						
9						
10	RECEPTION	MEAL	TOTAL MEAL COST	HORS D'OERVES	HORS	MEAL AND
11	MENU	PER PERSON	OF ALL GUESTS	PER PERSON	D'OERVES	HORS D'OERVES
12						
13	CHICKEN DIANE	42.50	4250.00	7.50	750.00	5000.00
14	SIRLOIN TIPS	47.50	4750.00	8.00	800.00	5550.00
15	PORK CHOPS	55.00	5500.00	8.50	850.00	6350.00
16	SURF AND TURF	66.75	6675.00	9.50	950.00	7625.00
17						
18						
19						
20	WALLINGFORD INN					
21						
22	RECEPTION	MEAL	TOTAL MEAL COST	HORS D'OERVES	HORS	MEAL AND
23	MENU	PER PERSON	OF ALL GUESTS	PER PERSON	D'OERVES	HORS D'OERVES
24						
25	CHICKEN DIANE	46.75		6.30		
26	SIRLOIN TIPS	49.00		7.00		
27	PORK CHOPS	54.50		7.50		
28	SURF AND TURF	68.75		8.25		
29						
30						
31						
32	ROMEO AND JULIET CASTLE INN					
33						
34	RECEPTION	MEAL	TOTAL MEAL COST	HORS D'OERVES	HORS	MEAL AND
35	MENU	PER PERSON	OF ALL GUESTS	PER PERSON	D'OERVES	HORS D'OERVES
36						
37	CHICKEN DIANE	50.50		7.25		
38	SIRLOIN TIPS	53.60		7.75		
39	PORK CHOPS	57.75		8.65		
40	SURF AND TURF	73.50		9.25		
41						
42	EXERCISE 45					
43	WEDDING					

Exercise 46 - Concepts Summary Exercise

SAVE AS: RECROOM

The Dinglehofer's have decided to redecorate their family room and they want to compute a Total amount for each item and a Total for the entire project. They have hired someone to do the work for them.

Directions

1. Plan this spreadsheet on the blank grid or enter it directly into the computer.

ITEM	UNITS	AMOUNT	PRICE
OAK PANELING	SHEETS	32	29.75
CARPETING	SQ. YARDS	34	27.5
CEILING TILES	TILES	29	9.89
LIGHTS	FIXTURES	6	32.9
WALL OUTLETS	OUTLETS	4	5.99
WIRING	FEET	100	.89
DOORS		2	112
FLOOR TILES	EACH	120	8.9
SOFA		1	790
CHAIRS	EACH	2	320
TELEVISION		1	450
END TABLES	EACH	2	170
CABLE HOOKUP		1	100
BOOK SHELVES	EACH	2	275
NAILS	POUNDS	5	2.5

2. Enter a formula to compute the following:
   TOTAL PAID for each item. (Ex: What they paid for paneling, carpeting, etc.)
   TOTAL of the TOTAL PAID for *all* items (use a function).
3. In addition to materials, the Dingelhofer's will pay $10 per hour for labor. It will take 10 hours to install the paneling, 5 hours for the carpeting, 3 hours for electricity, and 7 hours for miscellaneous. Enter a formula to show GRAND TOTAL. (The GRAND TOTAL is what it will cost them for the entire redecorating job – including labor.)
4. SAVE AS: RECROOM and print.

	A	B	C	D	E	F	G	H
1								
2								
3								
4								
5								
6								
7								
8								
9								
10								
11								
12								
13								
14								
15								
16								
17								
18								
19								
20								
21								
22								
23								
24								
25								
26								
27								

Exercise 47 - Concepts Summary Exercise

SAVE AS: SPORT

As owner of Forrest Football's Sporting Goods Store, you want to keep track of the weekly sales of each salesperson on your staff. They are paid solely on commission and *do not* receive a base salary. They earn a different percent commission for each department.

In the *sports department*, the commission earned is *15 percent* of their total sales; in the *exercise department*, the commission earned is *10 percent* of their total sales and in the *camping and fishing department*, the commission earned is *12 percent* of their total sales.

HELPFUL HINTS

- ➔ Use functions as much as possible.
- ➔ Create a column for commission percents.
- ➔ Divide into three departments.
- ➔ If you choose to plan this spreadsheet on a grid, you will need another copy of a grid because this is a large spreadsheet.

Directions

1. Enter your spreadsheet directly into the computer or plan it on one or two blank grids for FORREST FOOTBALL'S SPORTING GOODS STORE.
2. Divide this spreadsheet into 3 departments. (Use days of the week as column headings).
3. On the grid, write formulas to compute the following:

   TOTAL, AVERAGE, MINIMUM, and MAXIMUM SALES for each salesperson in each department.
   TOTAL, AVERAGE, MINIMUM and MAXIMUM SALES for each day of the week (Monday, Tuesday, etc.) for each department.

4. Copy all formulas appropriately.

5. Enter a PERCENT of COMMISSION column.
6. Enter a formula for TOTAL SALES for each department.
7. Write a formula for SALARY (Percent of Commission x Total Sales) for each salesperson.
8. Enter a GRAND TOTAL of SALES for all *three* departments.

SPORTS DEPARTMENT

1. Johnson, K: Monday, 534.67; Tuesday, 392.87; Wednesday, 199.98; Thursday, 234.55; Friday, 322.99.
2. Martindale, A: Monday, 444.55; Tuesday, 211.34; Wednesday, 119.00; Thursday, 432.88; Friday, 566.99.
3. Shillingsburg, T: Monday, 322.67; Tuesday, 165.00; Wednesday, 543.89; Thursday, 233.54; Friday, 676.00.

EXERCISE DEPARTMENT

1. Gray, B: Monday, 790.89; Tuesday, 345.67; Wednesday, 870.87; Thursday, 432.44; Friday, 322.78.
2. Cellini, A: Monday, 989.77; Tuesday, 345.45; Wednesday, 765.87; Thursday, 266.54; Friday, 901.76.

CAMPING AND FISHING DEPARTMENT

1. Andrews, J: Monday, 344.32; Tuesday, 233.56; Wednesday, 444.98; Thursday, 767.99; Friday, 540.00.
2. Feinstein, R: Monday, 876.99; Tuesday, 666.98; Wednesday, 543.22; Thursday, 767.00; Friday, 231.99.
3. Higgins, L: Monday, 456.88; Tuesday, 565.88; Wednesday, 333.90; Thursday, 565.90; Friday, 555.87.

8. SAVE AS: SPORT.
9. Print. (This will print on two or three pages.)

	A	B	C	D	E	F	G	H
1								
2								
3								
4								
5								
6								
7								
8								
9								
10								
11								
12								
13								
14								
15								
16								
17								
18								
19								
20								
21								
22								
23								
24								
25								
26								
27								

UNIT 6

Concepts:

Formatting
Inserting Rows and Columns
Deleting Rows and Columns
Copying
Relative and Absolute Formulas

Points to Remember:

➲ Formatting cells only changes the appearance of the cell. It does not affect calculating formulas.

➲ Formatting adds commas, dollar signs, or percents to values plus a variety of other appearance changes.

➲ You can format a single cell or a range of cells.

➲ Some software programs have WYSIWYG for formatting. This means "what you see is what you get." What you see on your screen is the way the spreadsheet will print as long as the printer is loaded with all of the necessary fonts, etc.

➲ The formatting of a cell can be copied from cell to cell.

➲ When inserting or deleting rows or columns, check the location of your cell pointer before you bring up the menu.

➲ When *inserting* rows and columns, the formulas usually adjust so they can continue to refer to the correct cell.

➲ If any rows or columns are deleted that contain cell addresses directly in a formula, you may get an Error message.

➲ If an ERR (error) message appears on the screen, retype the formula and copy it.

➲ Always save your model *before deleting* rows or columns.

➲ If you insert or delete the wrong row or column, try *Undo* immediately.

Exercise 48 - Formatting Values, Formulas

RESAVE AS: MYBUDGET

You would like to add more information to your personal budget of income and expenses. You are also interested in a savings plan with the available funds after your expenses.

HELPFUL HINTS

- ➔ Miscellaneous income might be earnings from stocks, savings, etc.
- ➔ The formula in cell E36 shows how much money you would need to keep as spending money for 11 days at $20 a day. You need to keep this amount and not put it into savings.
- ➔ This may print on two pages.

Directions

1. Retrieve MYBUDGET.
2. Erase the file name and exercise number.
3. Widen column A to 37 spaces.
4. Enter MISCELLANEOUS INCOME in A5, TOTAL AVAILABLE in A7, TOTAL EXPENSES in A30, and TOTAL AVAILABLE AFTER EXPENSES in cell A32 and 290 in E5.
5. Enter a formula in E7, E30, and E32.
6. Type NUMBER OF DAYS TO NEXT PAYCHECK in cell A34.
7. Enter the value 11 in cell E34.
8. Type DAILY EXPENSES @20 PER DAY in A36.
9. Enter a formula in E36 (NUMBER OF DAYS x 20).
10. Type TOTAL AVAILABLE FOR SAVINGS in A38.
11. Enter a formula in E38.
12. Format all money as currency with zero decimals.
13. Retype file name and adjust the exercise number on the spreadsheet.
14. RESAVE AS: MYBUDGET.
15. Print.

	A	B	C	D	E
1	MONTHLY BUDGET FOR MONTH OF				JANUARY
2					
3	INCOME				
4	MONTHLY PAYCHECK				$2,011
5	MISCELLANEOUS INCOME				$290
6					
7	TOTAL AVAILABLE				
8					
9					
10	EXPENSES				
11					
12	MORTGAGE				$475
13	CAR PAYMENT				$236
14	GAS FOR CAR				$55
15	TELEPHONE				$49
16	WATER				$39
17	SEWAGE				$30
18	CABLE				$25
19	ELECTRIC				$109
20	VISA				$80
21	MASTERCARD				$140
22	LACY'S				$60
23	INSURANCE--HEALTH				$290
24	DOCTOR BILLS				$45
25	DENTIST BILLS				$0
26	WAGE TAX				$22
27	INSURANCE--HOUSE				$280
28	OTHER				$79
29					
30	TOTAL EXPENSES				
31					
32	TOTAL AVAILABLE AFTER EXPENSES				
33					
34	NUMBER OF DAYS TO NEXT PAYCHECK				11
35					
36	DAILY EXPENSES@20 PER DAY				
37					
38	TOTAL AVAILABLE FOR SAVINGS				
39					
40					
41	MYBUDGET				
42	EXERCISE 48				

Exercise 49 - Formatting, Functions, Copying

RESAVE AS: COMMISS

Formatting this spreadsheet will improve its appearance. The agency would also like to compute the averages, minimum and maximum for Commission, Base Salary, and Total Salary.

HELPFUL HINTS

➔ When formatting cells for currency, you may see asterisks or other symbols in the cells; simply widen the column to see the values.
➔ In column D .06 will appear as a percent on the screen.

Directions

1. Retrieve COMMISS.
2. Erase cells A18 and A19.
3. Type the word AVERAGE in cell A18, MINIMUM in cell A19 and MAXIMUM in A20.
4. In cell E18, enter a function to show AVERAGE COMMISSION.
5. Copy the function from E18 to F18..G18.
6. In cell E19, enter a function to show MINIMUM COMMISSION.
7. Copy the function from E19 to F19..G19.
8. In cell E20, enter a function to show MAXIMUM COMMISSION.
9. Copy the function from E20 to F20..G20.
10. Format the values in column D as percent with no decimals. (This will only be necessary in some software applications.)
11. Format the values in column C, E, F and G as currency with no decimals.
12. Retype the file name and the exercise number.
13. RESAVE AS: COMMISS.
14. Print.

	A	B	C	D	E	F	G
1	CALDERI'S REAL ESTATE						
2	COMMISSION REPORT						
3	WEEK ENDING MAY 30, 1996						
4							
5				COMM.			TOTAL
6	AGENT	LOCATION	SALES	RATE	COMMISSION	BASE SALARY	SALARY
7							
8	LOCKWOOD	LOGANWOOD	$987,000	6%	$59,220	$1,500	$60,720
9	DEADY	THORNBURY	$634,000	6%	$38,040	$1,500	$39,540
10	BELSASCO	PINEHURST	$854,000	6%	$51,240	$1,500	$52,740
11	SOSTMANN	WILLOUGHBY	$550,000	6%	$33,000	$1,500	$34,500
12	POWELL	LOGANWOOD	$654,000	6%	$39,240	$1,500	$40,740
13	WHITMORE	PINEHURST	$439,000	6%	$26,340	$1,500	$27,840
14	SONG	MONACO	$689,000	6%	$41,340	$1,500	$42,840
15	COAKLEY	THORNBURY	$320,000	6%	$19,200	$1,500	$20,700
16							
17	TOTAL				$307,620	$12,000	$319,620
18	AVERAGE						
19	MINIMUM						
20	MAXIMUM						
21							
22	COMMISS						
23	EXERCISE 49						

Notes:

Exercise 50 - Formatting, Functions, Copying

RESAVE AS: FRUIT

John is ready to compute his total profit for the week ending July 16, 1995.

HELPFUL HINTS

- ➔ Always save the spreadsheet before inserting or deleting a row or column.
- ➔ Formatting cells can be done before or after the values are entered.
- ➔ Adjust column widths as necessary.

Directions

1. Retrieve FRUIT.
2. Enter all the column headings in cells F4, F5, G4, G5, H4, H5.
3. Enter TOTAL in A18, AVERAGE in A19, LOWEST in A20, and HIGHEST in A21.
4. Enter values in column F as shown.
5. Enter a formula in G7 to show SELLING PRICE TOTAL (SELLING PRICE per UNIT x AMOUNT SOLD).
6. Copy the formula from G7 to G8..G16.
7. Enter a formula in H7 to show TOTAL PROFIT.
8. Copy the formula from H7 to H8..H16.
9. Enter a function in E18 to show TOTAL for TOTAL COST.
10. Copy the formula from E18 to F18..H18.
11. Enter a function in E19 to show AVERAGE for TOTAL COST.
12. Copy the formula from E19 to F19..H19.
13. Enter a function in E20 to show LOWEST for TOTAL COST.
14. Copy the formula from E20 to F20..H20.
15. Enter a function in E21 to show HIGHEST for TOTAL COST.
16. Copy the formula from E21 to F21..H21.
17. Format all values in columns D, E, F, G, and H for currency with 2 decimals.
18. RESAVE AS: FRUIT and Print.

	A	B	C	D	E	F	G	H
1		JOHN'S FRESH FRUIT						
2		WEEK ENDING JULY 16, 1995						
3								
4			AMOUNT	COST	TOTAL	SELLING PRICE	SELLING PRICE	TOTAL
5	PRODUCT	UNITS	SOLD	PER UNIT	COST	PER UNIT	TOTAL	PROFIT
6								
7	BANANAS	POUND	17	$0.20	$3.40	$0.63		
8	PLUMS	POUND	26	$0.19	$4.94	$0.75		
9	PEACHES	POUND	29	$0.12	$3.48	$0.39		
10	CHERRIES	PINT	19	$0.33	$6.27	$0.89		
11	PEARS	POUND	9	$0.22	$1.98	$0.67		
12	KIWI	EACH	17	$0.20	$3.40	$0.75		
13	GRAPEFRUIT	EACH	23	$0.14	$3.22	$0.39		
14	HONEYDEW	EACH	13	$0.44	$5.72	$0.99		
15	CANTELOUPE	EACH	19	$0.30	$5.70	$0.79		
16	NECTARINES	POUND	19	$0.28	$5.32	$0.99		
17								
18	TOTAL							
19	AVERAGE							
20	LOWEST							
21	HIGHEST							
22	FRUIT							
23	EXERCISE 50							

Notes:

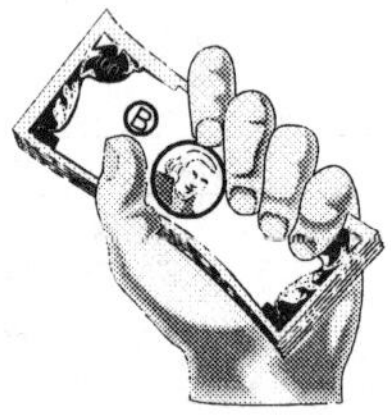

Exercise 51 - Formatting, Inserting and Deleting Rows, Copying

RESAVE AS: SALARY

You need to update your employee salary report.

HELPFUL HINTS

- ➔ If you delete or insert the wrong row or column, immediately use the *Undo* feature.
- ➔ To insert a row or a column, put your cell pointer where you want the new row or column to be and then insert.

Directions

1. Retrieve SALARY.
2. RICHARD FASSETT has quit; delete row 8.
3. TRACY COLEMAN has also quit; delete row 9.
4. Insert a new row 9. Type the following information in row 9: POLINOWSKI, SUSAN; 997-89-2343; 11/12/92; 40; and 14.75.
5. Copy the formula from F8 into F9; from G8 into G9; from H8 into H9, and from I8 into I9.
6. Insert a new row 12. Add the following information in row 12: GRAILNICK, SHIRLEY; 411-12-0070; 2/22/94; 27; and 10.35.
7. Copy the formula from F11 into F12; from G11 to G12; from H11 to H12, and from I11 to I12.
8. Insert a new row 14. Add the following information in row 14: SCHER, EVELYN; 547-76-3211; 8/9/94; 30; and 15.25.
9. Copy the formula from F13 into F14, from G13 to G14, from H13 to H14 and from I13 to I14.
10. Check the formulas in rows 18, 19, 20, and 21 and make sure they have adapted to their new location.

11. Format columns E, F, G, H, and I for currency with 2 decimal places and format column D for number or fixed with no decimal places.
12. Check the formulas in columns G, H, and I.
13. If all formulas have adapted to their new location, save the spreadsheet. If all formulas have not adapted to their new location, re-enter the formulas and check for accuracy.
14. Adjust the exercise number.
15. RESAVE AS: SALARY.
16. Print.

	A	B	C	D	E	F	G	H	I
1	SALARY REPORT								
2	WEEK ENDING MAY 3(	, 1995							
3									
4		SOCIAL SECURITY	DATE	TOTAL	HOURLY	GROSS			
5	NAME	NUMBER	HIRED	HOURS	RATE	PAY	F.W.T.	S.S.T.	NET PAY
6									
7	THOMPSON, JAMES	123-78-9087	1/14/82	40	$9.25	$370.00			
8	HIBBERD, BETSY	665-65-7654	6/5/88	35	$12.65	$442.75			
9	POLINOWSKI, SUSAN	997-89-2343	11/12/92	40	$14.75				
10	ROYCHOUD, ALBERT	342-76-9981	5/17/69	47	$22.67	$1,065.49			
11	ALYANAKIAN, LOUIS	357-63-0070	12/19/83	32	$11.55	$369.60			
12	GRAILNICK, SHIRLEY	411-12-0070	2/22/95	27	$10.35				
13	WHEAT, CINDERELLA	769-31-5432	4/29/80	40	$13.95	$558.00			
14	SCHER, EVELYN	547-76-3211	8/9/94	30	$15.25				
15	THOMPSON, CHRIS	231-98-6665	5/23/95	44	$7.75	$341.00			
16	GREY, EVELYN	665-01-0041	5/25/95	36	$8.10	$291.60			
17									
18	TOTAL								
19	AVERAGE								
20	MINIMUM								
21	MAXIMUM								
22									
23	SALARY								
24	EXERCISE 51								
25									

Notes:

Exercise 52 - Deleting a Row, Formatting, Printing

RESAVE AS: WEDDING

Michael and Vanessa would like to improve the appearance of their spreadsheet.

HELPFUL HINTS

- ➔ Follow the directions in order.
- ➔ Be careful when deleting rows or columns — make sure your cell pointer is in the correct row or column before choosing delete.

Directions

1. Retrieve WEDDING.
2. Delete row 3.
3. Keep 100 in D4 for the amount of guests.
4. Format all values in columns B, C, D, E and F for currency with two decimals.
5. RESAVE AS: WEDDING.
6. Print.

	A	B	C	D	E	F
1		MICHAEL AND VANESSA'S WEDDING				
2		RECEPTION ARRANGEMENTS				
3						
4	AMOUNT OF GUESTS			100		
5						
6						
7	MONT CHATEAU RESTAURANT					
8						
9	RECEPTION	MEAL	TOTAL MEAL COST	HORS D'OERVES	TOTAL	MEAL AND
10	MENU	PER PERSON	OF ALL GUESTS	PER PERSON	HORS D'OERVES	HORS D'OERVES
11						
12	CHICKEN DIANE	$42.50	$4,250.00	$7.50	$750.00	$5,000.00
13	SIRLOIN TIPS	$47.50	$4,750.00	$8.00	$800.00	$5,550.00
14	PORK CHOPS	$55.00	$5,500.00	$8.50	$850.00	$6,350.00
15	SURF/TURF	$66.75	$6,675.00	$9.50	$950.00	$7,625.00
16						
17						
18	WALLINGFORD INN					
19						
20	RECEPTION	MEAL	TOTAL MEAL COST	HORS D'OERVES	TOTAL	MEAL AND
21	MENU	PER PERSON	OF ALL GUESTS	PER PERSON	HORS D'OERVES	HORS D'OERVES
22						
23	CHICKEN DIANE	$46.75	$4,675.00	$6.30	$630.00	$5,305.00
24	SIRLOIN TIPS	$49.00	$4,900.00	$7.00	$700.00	$5,600.00
25	PORK CHOPS	$54.50	$5,450.00	$7.50	$750.00	$6,200.00
26	SURF/TURF	$68.75	$6,875.00	$8.25	$825.00	$7,700.00
27						
28						
29	ROMEO AND JULIET CASTLE INN					
30						
31	RECEPTION	MEAL	TOTAL MEAL COST	HORS D'OERVES	TOTAL	MEAL AND
32	MENU	PER PERSON	OF ALL GUESTS	PER PERSON	HORS D'OERVES	HORS D'OERVES
33						
34	CHICKEN DIANE	$50.50	$5,050.00	$7.25	$725.00	$5,775.00
35	SIRLOIN TIPS	$53.60	$5,360.00	$7.75	$775.00	$6,135.00
36	PORK CHOPS	$57.75	$5,775.00	$8.65	$865.00	$6,640.00
37	SURF/TURF	$73.50	$7,350.00	$9.25	$925.00	$8,275.00
38						
39	WEDDING					
40	EXERCISE 52					

Exercise 53 - Functions, (Sum, Average, Minimum, Maximum, Count), Absolute Formulas, Formatting

SAVE AS: JEWELRY

The Myers Discount Jewelry Store is pricing specific pieces of jewelry from Merv's Wholesale House of Jewelry.

Directions

1. Enter the spreadsheet as shown.
2. When typing the values as percents in column C, type them as percents. Simply type 240%. It will appear as a decimal. This also applies to B4.
3. Format the values in column C and B4 as percents with no decimal.
4. Enter a formula in D9 to compute SELLING PRICE (MARKUP x COST OF ITEM).
5. Copy the formula from D9 to D10..D19.
6. Enter a formula in E9 to compute SALES TAX paid.
7. Copy the formula from E9 to E10..E19.
8. Enter a formula in F9 to compute TOTAL PRICE.
9. Copy the formula from F9 to F10..F19.
10. Enter a function in B21 to compute TOTAL of COST PER ITEM.
11. Copy the formula from B21 to D21..F21.
12. Enter a function in B22 to compute AVERAGE of COST PER ITEM.
13. Copy the function from B22 to D22..F22.
14. Enter a function in B23 to compute LOWEST of COST PER ITEM.
15. Copy the function from B23 to D23..F23.
16. Enter a function in B24 to compute HIGHEST of COST PER ITEM.
17. Copy the function from B24 to D24..F24.
18. Enter a function in B25 to show NUMBER OF ITEMS.
19. Format columns B, D, E and F for currency with two decimals (except for B25).
20. Format B25 as a whole number.
21. SAVE AS: JEWELRY.
22. Print.

	A	B	C	D	E	F
1	BEST DISCOUNT JEWELRY					
2	MERV'S WHOLESALE JEWELRY					
3						
4	SALES TAX:	8%				
5						
6		COST	MARKUP	SELLING	SALES	TOTAL
7	ITEM	PER ITEM		PRICE	TAX	PRICE
8						
9	ONYX RING	$99	240%			
10	DIAMOND BRACELET	$290	600%			
11	SWISS WATCH	$240	425%			
12	RUBY TIARA	$400	700%			
13	GOLD ROPE CHAIN	$200	425%			
14	TURQUOISE RING	$190	490%			
15	EMERALD WATCH	$359	600%			
16	PEARL BRACELET	$202	250%			
17	OPAL RING	$349	350%			
18	ONYX BRACELET	$130	200%			
19	RUBY NECKLACE	$500	390%			
20						
21	TOTAL					
22	AVERAGE					
23	LOWEST					
24	HIGHEST					
25	NUMBER OF ITEMS					
26						
27	JEWELRY					
28	EXERCISE 53					

Notes:

Exercise 54 - Functions, Copying, Formatting

SAVE AS: ENGLISH

Miss Tia Cher would like to compute averages for her English class. Test averages and spelling averages will be kept separate in this spreadsheet.

HELPFUL HINTS

➔ Only use functions in this spreadsheet.
➔ In cell D14, enter the zero; do not leave the cell blank.
➔ Widen and narrow columns as necessary.

Directions

1. Enter the spreadsheet as shown.
2. Center all column headings.
3. Using a function in cell E6, compute the TEST AVERAGE for Robert Anders.
4. Copy the formula from E6 into E7..E19.
5. Using a function in cell H6, compute the SPELLING AVERAGE for Robert Anders.
6. Copy the formula from H6 into H7..H19.
7. Format columns E and H as numbers with no decimal places.
8. SAVE AS: ENGLISH.
9. Print.

	A	B	C	D	E	F	G	H
1	MISS TIA CHER							
2	ENGLISH							
3								
4		TEST 1	TEST 2	TEST 3	TEST AVG.	SPELLING 1	SPELLING 2	SPELLING AVG.
5								
6	ANDERS, ROBERT	97	95	91		88	96	
7	BROTHERSTON, JOHN	97	100	97		100	100	
8	BENJAMIN, MARIE	91	90	100		96	96	
9	CLEVELAND, ELYSE	94	100	95		96	88	
10	CRONIN, KURT	100	100	100		72	100	
11	WHITBY, SUSAN	97	95	100		100	100	
12	DAVIS, SARAH	100	100	100		100	100	
13	HARRISON, BARBARA	97	100	100		96	96	
14	McFERSON, CONNIE	82	85	0		80	88	
15	MITCHELL, DAVID	81	95	100		84	92	
16	PERICELLI, ANTHONY	80	100	100		96	100	
17	RICHARDSON, LESLIE	97	100	100		72	96	
18	SANTINI, MICHAEL	70	75	93		60	88	
19	ZIMMERS, WILLIAM	91	95	96		96	100	
20								
21	ENGLISH							
22	EXERCISE 54							

Notes:

Exercise 55 - Concepts Summary Exercise

SAVE AS: TOY

The owner of Fun Toys, Inc. is in the process of comparing wholesale prices from three separate wholesalers for several popular toys. She will buy all the items from *one* wholesaler *only*. After the spreadsheet is completed, decide which of the three wholesalers she should purchase the toys from for her store for the Christmas holiday. Choose *one* wholesaler.

Directions

1. Create a spreadsheet on a copy of a grid, or you may enter the spreadsheet directly into the computer.
2. Separate each wholesaler on the spreadsheet.

TOY	A-1 WHOLESALE COMPANY	WHOLESALE GOODS INC.	WHOLESALE HOUSE OF TOYS
Mighty Max	3.00	3.25	3.90
Baby Bonnie	13.00	11.50	12.40
Bubble Baby	10.74	9.00	10.00
Dinosaur Fred	5.75	5.75	6.25
Sticker Suzie	9.80	9.25	8.90
Ultimate Construction	35.00	36.00	39.00
Jumpin' Joe	9.25	8.00	7.80
Stinker Toys	12.80	12.00	14.00

3. Each wholesale house will be giving you a discount for each item as follows: A-1 WHOLESALE DISCOUNT is 12%; WHOLESALE GOODS INC. is 10%; and the WHOLESALE HOUSE of TOYS is 8%.
4. Create a horizontal window if necessary to enter remaining information.
5. After entering the information in three separate areas, create a column for DISCOUNT and another column for TOTAL COST.
6. Enter all formulas and copy.
7. Also compute a TOTAL amount for WHOLESALE COST, DISCOUNT and TOTAL COST for each wholesale company.
8. Using TOTAL COST, choose which wholesaler has the best offer.
9. Format all values as currency with 2 decimals.
10. SAVE AS: TOY and Print.

	A	B	C	D	E	F	G	H
1								
2								
3								
4								
5								
6								
7								
8								
9								
10								
11								
12								
13								
14								
15								
16								
17								
18								
19								
20								
21								
22								
23								
24								
25								
26								
27								

Exercise 56 - Concepts Summary Exercise

SAVE AS: PAINTJOB

Your car needs a new paint job and you have decided to get two estimates from two different paint shops in the area—Payco's Paint and Repair Shop and Painting, Painting, Painting.

Directions

1. Write the information below on the grid to create a spreadsheet or enter it directly into the computer.

Payco's Paint and Repair Shop		Painting, Painting, Painting	
JOB	Hours	JOB	Hours
SANDING	3	SANDING	3
MINOR REPAIRS	3	MINOR REPAIRS	2
PRIMER	1	PRIMER	1
PAINTING	3	PAINTING	4
FINISH COAT	2	FINISH COAT	3
Total Hours		Total Hours	

2. The labor rate for PAYCO'S PAINT and REPAIR SHOP is $15 PER HOUR. Enter a formula to compute the TOTAL LABOR costs for each job and another formula for the entire painting job (TOTAL ESTIMATE). Also enter a formula for TOTAL HOURS. Use an *absolute* formula.
3. The labor rate for PAINTING, PAINTING, PAINTING is $12 PER HOUR. Enter a formula to compute the TOTAL LABOR costs for each job and another formula for the entire painting job (TOTAL ESTIMATE). Also enter a formula for TOTAL HOURS. Use an *absolute* formula. Copy the formulas as much as possible.
4. Check your individual prices and make sure that the charges add up to the total estimate.
5. Format the values accordingly.
6. Which company has the better deal?
7. SAVE AS: PAINTJOB.
8. Print.

	A	B	C	D	E	F	G	H
1								
2								
3								
4								
5								
6								
7								
8								
9								
10								
11								
12								
13								
14								
15								
16								
17								
18								
19								
20								
21								
22								
23								
24								
25								
26								
27								

Competencies:

After completing this unit, you will know how to:

1. Format cells
2. Insert rows and columns
3. Delete rows and columns
4. Copy labels, values and formulas
5. Enter relative and absolute formulas
6. Develop functions

UNIT 7

Concepts:

Fixing or Freezing Titles
Windows (Splitting the Screen)
Formatting
Inserting Rows and Columns
Deleting Rows and Columns
Functions
Cutting and Pasting (Move)

Points to Remember:

- Since the topmost rows and columns are often used for identifying contents of rows and columns, scrolling can make them temporarily disappear from the screen. You can fix titles so that the rest of the model scrolls under them.
- In some spreadsheet programs, you cannot edit the part of the spreadsheet that is fixed or frozen.
- Windows split your screen into two vertical or horizontal parts.
- You can edit in either window when the screen is split.
- Cutting and pasting (moving) is extremely useful when moving a single cell, a column, a row or a range.
- Be careful when cutting and pasting (moving) formulas. Check for any Error messages. If you see an ERR message, simply retype the correct formula and recopy.
- When performing a cut and paste, if there is any information in the target range, it will be overridden by the new information.
- Always save before you cut and paste (move) any data.

Exercise 57 - Freezing Titles, Copying, Formatting

RESAVE AS: EXPENSES

The Sweets Candy Company wants to look at years six, seven and eight for projected expenses.

HELPFUL HINTS

- ➔ If a cell fills with asterisks or other symbols, widen the column until the values are visible.
- ➔ When you freeze or fix column A, you should be in column B.

Directions

1. Retrieve EXPENSES.
2. Freeze or Fix titles in column B.
3. Type YEAR 5 in cell F6, YEAR 6 in G6, YEAR 7 in H6, and YEAR 8 in I6.
4. Copy the formula from E8 to F8.
5. Copy the formula from F8 to F9..F13.
6. Copy the formula from F8 to G8.
7. Copy the formula from G8 to G9..G13.
8. Copy the formula from G8 to H8.
9. Copy the formula from H8 to H9..H13.
10. Copy the formula from H8 to I8.
11. Copy the formula from I8 to I9..I13.
12. Copy the formula from E15 to F15..I15.
13. Format all values as currency with two decimals.
14. Clear the titles.
15. RESAVE AS: EXPENSES.

	A	B	C	D
1	PROJECTION OF BUSINESS EXPENSES			
2	SWEETS CANDY COMPANY			
3				
4	ANNUAL INCREASE RATE:	6.25%		
5				
6	EXPENSES	YEAR 1	YEAR 2	YEAR 3
7				
8	RENT	$14,567.00		
9	UTILITIES	$1,198.00		
10	MACHINERY UPKEEP	$1,010.00		
11	SALARIES	$387,000.00		
12	ADVERTISING	$8,235.00		
13	DELIVERY/FREIGHT	$1,500.00		
14				
15	TOTAL			
16				
17	EXPENSES			
18	EXERCISE 57			

	E	F	G	H	I
1					
2					
3					
4					
5					
6	YEAR 4	YEAR 5	YEAR 6	YEAR 7	YEAR 8
7					
8					
9					
10					
11					
12					
13					
14					
15					
16					
17					
18					

Exercise 58 - Formulas, Windows, Printing

RESAVE AS: INCOME

Lacy's Department Store is still in the process of investigating its growth and it would like to see Net Income or Loss for three years.

Directions

1. Retrieve INCOME.
2. Create a vertical window in column B.
3. Enter the new information for the second and third year.
4. Copy the formula from B8 to D8 and F8.
5. Copy the formula from B15 to D15 and F15.
6. Copy the formula from B17 to D17 and F17.
7. Copy the formula from B25 to D25 and F25.
8. Copy the formula from B28 to D28 and F28.
9. Copy the formula from B31 to D31 and F31.
10. Delete any zeros in column E.
11. Format all values for currency with no decimals.
12. Erase cell A1 and retype LACY'S INCOME STATEMENT in B1.
13. Clear the window.
14. RESAVE AS: INCOME.
15. Print.

	A	B	C	D	E	F
1		LACY'S INCOME STATEMENT				
2						
3						
4	SALES	1ST YEAR		2ND YEAR		3RD YEAR
5						
6	GROSS SALES	$79,665		$99,677		$113,901
7	RETURNS	$1,754		$3,456		$5,334
8	NET SALES	$77,911				
9						
10						
11	COST OF GOODS SOLD					
12						
13	PURCHASE PRICE	$39,844		$48,221		$59,000
14	FREIGHT	$2,002		$4,211		$3,555
15	TOTAL COST OF GOOD SOLD	$41,846				
16						
17	GROSS PROFIT	$36,065				
18						
19						
20	OPERATING COSTS					
21						
22	INTEREST	$19,000		$24,456		$22,789
23	ADMINISTRATIVE	$4,052		$5,677		$5,099
24	DEPRECIATION	$2,054		$2,231		$2,030
25	TOTAL OPERATING COSTS	$25,106				
26						
27						
28	OPERATING INCOME BEFORE TAXES	$10,959				
29	TAXES	$3,998		$4,212		$4,212
30						
31	NET INCOME/LOSS	$6,961				
32						
33	INCOME					
34	EXERCISE 58					

Exercise 59 - Formatting, Inserting, Copying

RESAVE AS: BASEBALL

The little league baseball coach would like to include the Team Colors on his order. He will need to include this information in the following order.

Directions

1. Retrieve BASEBALL.
2. Erase cells A20 and A21.
3. Insert a blank column B.
4. Type TEAM COLOR in cell B4.
5. Enter the team colors as shown.
6. Type LOWEST in cell A19; HIGHEST in A20; and TOTAL TEAMS in A21.
7. Enter a function in C19 to compute the LOWEST amount of shirts ordered.
8. Copy the function from C19 to D19..G19.
9. Enter a function in C20 to compute the HIGHEST shirts.
10. Copy the function from C20 to D20..G20.
11. Enter a function in C21 to compute the TOTAL TEAMS.
12. Format all values as numbers with no decimals.
13. RESAVE AS: BASEBALL.
14. Print.

	A	B	C	D	E	F	G
1	LITTLE LEAGUE INVENTORY						
2	MAY, 1995						
3							
4	TEAM	TEAM COLOR	SHIRTS	PANTS	HATS	GLOVES	TOTAL
5							
6	BLUE JAYS	BLUE	23	21	23	9	76
7							
8	CARDINALS	RED	25	25	26	9	85
9							
10	HAWKS	BROWN	22	23	24	10	79
11							
12	EAGLES	WHITE	21	21	22	9	73
13							
14	FALCONS	GRAY	27	26	25	10	88
15							
16	RAVENS	BLACK	27	26	25	11	89
17							
18	TOTAL		145	142	145	58	490
19	LOWEST						
20	HIGHEST						
21	TOTAL TEAMS						
22							
23	BASEBALL						
24	EXERCISE 59						

Notes:

Exercise 60 - Formatting, Freezing Titles, Functions, Inserting, Printing

RESAVE AS: LUIGI

Luigi needs to be more specific on his inventory order. He will add specific colors for most of the items he needs.

Directions

1. Retrieve LUIGI.
2. Erase cell A48 and A49.
3. Insert a blank column B.
4. Go to row 6 and horizontally freeze titles.
5. Enter the following as shown in column B. There will be no color stated for the silverware.
6. In cell A47, type LOWEST.
7. In cell A48, type HIGHEST.
8. In cell A49, type NUMBER OF ITEMS.
9. Enter the functions in C47 to compute the LOWEST for COST PER ITEM and copy to D47..E47.
10. Enter the functions in C48 to compute the HIGHEST for COST PER ITEM and copy to D48..E48.
11. Enter a function in C49 for NUMBER OF ITEMS.
12. Format all values in column C and E as currency with two decimals, and format all values in column D as whole numbers.
13. Clear the titles.
14. RESAVE AS: LUIGI.
15. Print.

	A	B	C	D	E
1			LUIGI'S HOMEMADE PASTA PALACE		
2			NEW REMODELING INVENTORY		
3					
4			COST PER	NUMBER OF	TOTAL COST
5	ITEM	COLOR	ITEM	ITEMS	OF ITEMS
6					
7	SERVING PLATTERS	PINK FLOWERS	$22.55	45	$1,014.75
8					
9	NAPKINS	BURGUNDY	$2.35	100	$235.00
10					
11	CREAMERS	PINK	$5.67	50	$283.50
12					
13	PLACEMATS	GRAY	$5.75	50	$287.50
14					
15	SUGAR BOWLS	PINK	$5.67	15	$85.05
16					
17	TABLECLOTHS	BURGUNDY	$9.50	60	$570.00
18					
19	TABLE PADS	TAN	$11.00	30	$330.00
20					
21	SALAD BOWLS	PINK	$4.56	15	$68.40
22					
23	CANDLES FOR TABLES	BURGUNDY	$17.25	27	$465.75
24					
25	SALT SHAKERS	GRAY	$3.25	50	$162.50
26					
27	PEPPER SHAKERS	GRAY	$3.25	50	$162.50
28					
29	CHEESE SHAKERS	GRAY	$3.95	50	$197.50
30					
31	SILVERWARE (SERVICE 12)		$110.00	14	$1,540.00
32					
33	DISHES (SERVICE 12)	PINK FLOWERS	$97.00	14	$1,358.00
34					
35	SERVING SPOONS (SILVER)		$12.56	40	$502.40
36					
37	SERVING FORKS (SILVER)		$11.35	40	$454.00
38					
39	NAPKIN RINGS	GRAY	$2.95	100	$295.00
40					
41	ICE BUCKETS	SILVER	$7.65	30	$229.50
42					
43	HANGING FLOWERS	IVY	$55.65	12	$667.80
44					
45	TOTALS		$391.91	792	$8,909.15
46	AVERAGE		$20.63	42	$468.90
47	LOWEST				
48	HIGHEST				
49	NUMBER OF ITEMS				
50					
51	LUIGI				
52	EXERCISE 60				

Exercise 61 - Copying, Absolute Formulas, Windows, Formatting

RESAVE AS: MYBUDGET

Your boss has informed you that all of your hard work will be rewarded with a 2% raise for each month for the next three months. You also will be receiving a 2% bonus for each of the three months on your investments.

Directions

1. Retrieve MYBUDGET.
2. Enter the new information in F1, and G1 and H1.
3. Enter RAISE: in A2 and 2% in B2 and format B2 for percent with no decimals.
4. Create a vertical window in column C.
5. Enter a formula in F4 to compute the total raise increased by 2% for the month of February. Hint: This is an *absolute* formula. Remember to not only compute the raise but to add the monthly paycheck.
6. Copy the formula from F4 to G4..H4.
7. Enter a formula in F5 to compute the total increase in investments increased by 2%. Remember to not only compute the raise but to add the miscellaneous income.
8. Copy the formula from F5 to G5..H5.
9. Copy for formula from E7 to F7..H7.
10. Most of the expenses have remained the same. Copy the values from E12..E28 to F12..H28.
11. Make the following changes: TELEPHONE in FEBRUARY, $85; MARCH, $93; APRIL, $48. Use overtype to retype new information.
12. DENTIST expenses remain at 0 except for FEBRUARY which was $175.
13. Change the following values: OTHER in FEBRUARY, $99; MARCH, $67; APRIL, 140.
14. Copy the formula from E30 to F30..H30.
15. Copy the formula from E32 to F32..H32.
16. Enter the following values for NUMBER OF DAYS TO NEXT PAYCHECK: FEB., 11 (F34); MARCH, 8 (G34); APRIL, 11 (H34).
17. Copy the formula from E36 to F36..H36.
18. Copy the formula from E38 to F38..H38. Format all money as currency with no decimals. Format NUMBER OF DAYS TO NEXT PAYCHECK in row 34 as fixed with no decimals.

19. Copy the formula from E38 to F38..H38. Format all money as currency with no decimals. Format NUMBER OF DAYS TO NEXT PAYCHECK in row 34 as a whole number with no decimals.
20. Clear the window.
21. RESAVE AS: MYBUDGET.

	A	B	C	D	E	F	G	H
1	MONTHLY BUDGET FOR MONTH OF				JANUARY	FEBRUARY	MARCH	APRIL
2	RAISE:	2%						
3	TOTAL INCOME							
4	MONTHLY PAYCHECK				$2,011			
5	MISCELLANEOUS INCOME				$290			
6								
7	TOTAL AVAILABLE				$2,301			
8								
9								
10	TOTAL EXPENSES							
11								
12	MORTGAGE				$475			
13	CAR PAYMENT				$236			
14	GAS FOR CAR				$55			
15	TELEPHONE				$49			
16	WATER				$39			
17	SEWAGE				$30			
18	CABLE				$25			
19	ELECTRIC				$109			
20	VISA				$80			
21	MASTERCARD				$140			
22	LACY'S				$60			
23	INSURANCE--HEALTH				$290			
24	DOCTOR BILLS				$45			
25	DENTIST BILLS				$0			
26	WAGE TAX				$22			
27	INSURANCE--HOUSE				$280			
28	OTHER				$79			
29								
30	TOTAL EXPENSES				$2,014			
31								
32	TOTAL AVAILABLE AFTER EXPENSES				$287			
33								
34	NUMBER OF DAYS TO NEXT PAYCHECK				11			
35								
36	DAILY EXPENSES@20 PER DAY				$220			
37								
38	TOTAL AVAILABLE FOR SAVINGS				$67			
39								
40								
41	MYBUDGET							
42	EXERCISE 61							

Exercise 62 - Formulas, Functions, Copying, Printing

SAVE AS: SHOTS

The Norcross Basketball Team is beginning the process of compiling the records of four of their players for five games.

Directions

1. Enter the spreadsheet as shown.
2. Create a formula in F8 that shows TOTAL POINTS scored for each player for each game. (Remember that foul shots are worth one point and regular shots are worth two points each.)
3. Copy the formula from F8 to F9..F12 and from F12 to F16..F20 and from F20 to F24..F28 and from F28 to F32..F36.
4. Enter a function in F13 to show TOTAL POINTS scored for John Adamak.
5. Copy the function from F13 to F21 and from F21 to F29 and from F29 to F37.
6. Which player did the best?
7. SAVE AS: SHOTS.
8. Print the spreadsheet and circle the player who did the best.

	A	B	C	D	E	F
1	NORCROSS BASKETBALL RECORDS					
2	PRELIMINARY REPORT					
3						
4		SHOTS	SHOTS	FOUL SHOTS	FOUL SHOTS	TOTAL
5	PLAYER	ATTEMPTED	MADE	ATTEMPTED	MADE	POINTS
6						
7	ADAMAK, JOHN					
8	GAME 1	17	7	4	4	
9	GAME 2	11	9	2	1	
10	GAME 3	14	6	3	1	
11	GAME 4	9	6	4	0	
12	GAME 5	9	4	2	1	
13	5 GAME TOTAL					
14						
15	MOLESKY, BRAD					
16	GAME 1	11	8	2	2	
17	GAME 2	9	6	4	0	
18	GAME 3	6	0	2	0	
19	GAME 4	3	3	1	1	
20	GAME 5	4	2	2	1	
21	5 GAME TOTAL					
22						
23	MARTIN, JONATHAN					
24	GAME 1	8	7	6	3	
25	GAME 2	7	5	4	2	
26	GAME 3	7	1	0	0	
27	GAME 4	9	2	2	1	
28	GAME 5	11	5	2	0	
29	5 GAME TOTAL					
30						
31	SMITH, DARREN					
32	GAME 1	14	8	1	0	
33	GAME 2	11	3	2	0	
34	GAME 3	9	6	4	2	
35	GAME 4	5	4	4	0	
36	GAME 5	8	1	2	1	
37	5 GAME TOTAL					
38						
39	SHOTS					
40	EXERCISE 62					

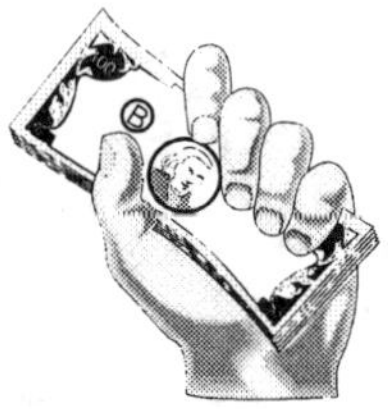

Exercise 63 - Formatting, Inserting, Deleting, Cutting and Pasting (Moving), Printing

RESAVE AS: SALARY

Insurance has now been added to the employees' deductions; therefore, the spreadsheet needs to be adjusted.

Directions

1. Retrieve SALARY.
2. Insert a blank column A.
3. Cut and paste (move) social security numbers from column C to the blank column A.
4. Widen column A if necessary.
5. Cut and paste (move) the labels from B18..B21 to A18..A21.
6. Delete the blank row 17.
7. Delete the blank column C.
8. Insert a blank column I.
9. Type INSURANCE in cell I5 and center it.
10. The INSURANCE deduction for everyone is $44.
11. Enter $44 in I7 and *copy* from I7 to I8..I16.
12. Adjust the formula in J7 to include the insurance deduction.
13. Copy the formula from J7 to J8..J16.
14. Copy the formulas from H17..H20 to I17..I20.
15. Copy the formulas from I17..I20 to J17..J20.
16. Format all money as currency with two decimals, and total hours as numbers with no decimals.
17. RESAVE AS: SALARY.
18. Print.

	A	B	C	D	E
1		SALARY REPORT			
2		WEEK ENDING MAY 30, 1995			
3					
4	SOCIAL SECURITY		DATE	TOTAL	HOURLY
5	NUMBER	NAME	HIRED	HOURS	RATE
6					
7	123-78-9087	THOMPSON, JAMES	1/14/82	40	$9.25
8	665-65-7654	HIBBERD, BETSY	6/5/88	35	$12.65
9	997-89-2343	POLINOWSKI, SUSAN	11/12/92	40	$14.75
10	342-76-9981	ROYCHOUD, ALBERT	5/17/69	47	$22.67
11	357-63-0070	ALYANAKIAN, LOUIS	12/19/83	32	$11.55
12	411-12-0700	GRAILNIK, SHIRLEY	2/22/94	27	$10.35
13	769-31-5432	WHEAT, CINDERELLA	4/29/80	40	$13.95
14	547-76-3211	SCHER, EVELYN	4/9/94	30	$15.25
15	231-98-6665	THOMPSON, CHRIS	5/23/95	44	$7.75
16	665-01-0041	GREY, EVELYN	5/25/95	36	$8.10
17	TOTAL			371	$126.27
18	AVERAGE			37	$12.63
19	LOWEST			27	$7.75
20	HIGHEST			47	$22.67
21					
22	SALARY				
23	EXERCISE 63				

	F	G	H	I	J
1					
2					
3					
4	GROSS				
5	PAY	F.W.T.	S.S.T.	INSURANCE	NET PAY
6					
7	$370.00	$74.00	$26.53	$44.00	
8	$442.75	$88.55	$31.75	$44.00	
9	$590.00	$118.00	$42.30	$44.00	
10	$1,065.49	$213.10	$76.40	$44.00	
11	$369.60	$73.92	$26.50	$44.00	
12	$279.45	$55.89	$20.04	$44.00	
13	$558.00	$111.60	$40.01	$44.00	
14	$457.50	$91.50	$32.80	$44.00	
15	$341.00	$68.20	$24.45	$44.00	
16	$291.60	$58.32	$20.91	$44.00	
17	$4,765.39	$953.08	$341.68		
18	$476.54	$95.31	$34.17		
19	$279.45	$55.89	$20.04		
20	$1,065.49	$213.10	$76.40		
21					
22					
23					

Exercise 64 - Concepts Summary Exercise

SAVE AS: SAT

George and Mary High School offers a full year SAT preparation course for students in their junior year. Students take one SAT test in their junior year before the SAT prep course. They take another SAT test in their senior year. The school would like to compare the SAT scores before and after the students' SAT preparation course.

Directions

1. Enter the information below into the grid or directly into the computer. Enter the information with no blank rows.

Student	Math SAT Scores Before the Course	Verbal SAT Score Before the Course	Math SAT Scores After the Course	Verbal SAT Scores After the Course
BILL WOOD	470	430	500	470
THERESA CHU	500	520	520	560
JIM CLARKE	610	530	620	560
BARRY GENKIN	490	580	510	590
LINDA DILUILLO	590	600	670	650
PAT O'LEARY	670	720	600	630
SEAN TUCK	460	480	520	510
CAROL HATCH	470	420	490	510
JOHN CICONE	430	500	540	550

4. Create a horizontal window to make it easier to enter the formulas below.
5. Create formulas to compute the following:
   TOTAL SAT SCORES (math plus verbal) before the course for each student.
   TOTAL SAT SCORES after the course for each student.
   AVERAGE MATH SAT SCORES before the course.
   AVERAGE VERBAL SAT SCORES before the course.
   AVERAGE MATH SAT SCORES after the course.
   AVERAGE VERBAL SAT SCORES after the course.
   DIFFERENCE IN TOTAL SAT SCORES before and after the course for each student.
   PERCENT of the INCREASE in TOTAL SAT SCORES from before to after the course for each student.
6. Clear the horizontal window.
7. SAVE AS: SAT and Print.
8. Insert a blank row between each students' name and print again.

	A	B	C	D	E	F	G	H
1								
2								
3								
4								
5								
6								
7								
8								
9								
10								
11								
12								
13								
14								
15								
16								
17								
18								
19								
20								
21								
22								
23								
24								
25								
26								
27								

Exercise 65 - Concepts Summary Exercise

SAVE AS: BIOLOGY

Mrs. Linda Shillingsburg has just finished grading her tenth grade Biology class finals. She would like to compute the students' final averages counting TEST 2 twice. Since most of her students did better on the second test than the first, this should bring up most of their grades.

Directions

1. Create a spreadsheet with the following information.

STUDENT	TEST 1	TEST 2	PROJECT 1	PROJECT 2	FINAL
COLIER, TOM	95	99	97	100	74
DART, SUSAN	87	89	91	90	80
BILLINGS, MONICA	99	100	87	96	86
DRAVO, DAWN	83	89	92	88	83
ADAMS, MEREDITH	99	97	100	98	94
GRASSA, STEVE	88	93	100	93	87
TIMM, ADRIENNE	90	95	90	73	78
LONG, JIM	73	77	61	80	62
MCCOY, JENNIFER	80	81	53	70	70
BEAUMONT, GREG	92	93	81	50	43
ROLAND, DAKOTA	99	100	54	99	80
LEX, KIRSTEN	72	84	81	90	77
WITHELDER, MANDY	90	91	87	99	88

2. Create a vertical window to insure accuracy when entering values.
3. Enter a formula for TEST AVERAGE (test 1 and test 2–one average). Enter a formula for PROJECT/FINAL AVERAGE (project 1, project 2 and final are one average).
4. Also enter an AVERAGE (all students) for TEST 1, TEST 2, PROJECT 1, PROJECT 2 and the FINAL.
5. Print.
6. Insert a blank column to the right of TEST 2 scores.
7. Copy TEST 2 scores into the blank column. TEST 2 will be counted twice to increase the students' FINAL GRADE. Check all formulas.
8. Enter a formula to compute FINAL GRADE. The TEST AVERAGE (total of 3 tests because test 2 will be counted twice) counts 50% of their grade and PROJECT/FINAL AVERAGE will also counts 50% of their final grade.
9. SAVE AS: BIOLOGY and print again.

	A	B	C	D	E	F	G	H
1								
2								
3								
4								
5								
6								
7								
8								
9								
10								
11								
12								
13								
14								
15								
16								
17								
18								
19								
20								
21								
22								
23								
24								
25								
26								
27								

Competencies:

After completing this unit, you will know how to:

1. Fix or freeze titles
2. Split the screen vertically and horizontally (windows)
3. Move a cell or a range of cells
4. Insert rows and columns
5. Delete rows and columns

UNIT 8

Concepts:

Changing the Model's Appearance
Bold
Underline
Shade
Italics
Changing Row Height
Borders
Colors
Landscape

Points to Remember:

- Shading and colors appear differently on the screen depending on the spreadsheet program.
- Landscape prints your spreadsheet horizontally.
- WYSIWYG means "What you see is what you get." WYSIWYG adds professional formatting.
- The formatting of a cell can be copied.
- If your spreadsheet is in color on your screen, you must have a color printer to view the hard copy in color.
- A *point* is a unit of measurement. The larger the point size, the larger the print.
- A *font* is a typeface – appearance of the type of print. For example: Script, Roman, Gothic.
- Usually formatting can be performed through a menu or an icon.
- Always use print preview (if applicable) before you print. Be aware of the page breaks in print preview.

Exercise 66 - Bold, Underline, Shade, Italic, Fonts

RESAVE AS: BASEBALL

You want to improve the appearance of this spreadsheet by bolding, shading, italicizing, and underlining.

Directions

1. Retrieve BASEBALL.
2. Italicize and bold the spreadsheet headings in rows 1 and 2.
3. Underline the text in row 1.
4. Bold and underline all column headings (TEAM, TEAM COLOR, etc.)
5. Shade the values in column G.
6. Shade the values in the range C18..G20 and C21.
7. Change the font of the entire spreadsheet.
8. Resave as: BASEBALL.

	A	B	C	D	E	F	G
1	***LITTLE LEAGUE INVENTORY***						
2	***MAY, 1995***						
3							
4	**TEAM**	**TEAM NO.**	**SHIRTS**	**PANTS**	**HATS**	**GLOVES**	**TOTAL**
5							
6	BLUE JAYS	12	23	21	23	9	
7							
8	CARDINALS	17	25	25	26	9	
9							
10	HAWKS	11	22	23	24	10	
11							
12	EAGLES	9	21	21	22	9	
13							
14	FALCONS	14	27	26	25	10	
15							
16	RAVENS	6	27	26	25	11	
17							
18	TOTAL						
19	LOWEST						
20	HIGHEST						
21	TOTAL TEAMS						
22							
23	BASEBALL						
24	EXERCISE 66						

Notes:

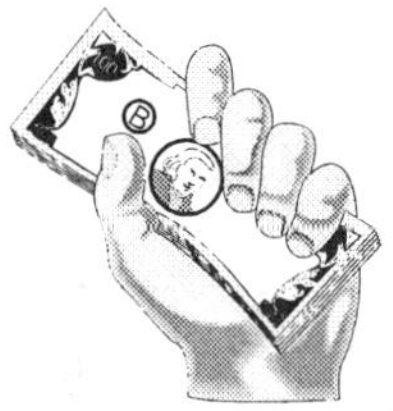

Exercise 67 - Centering the Heading Across the Spreadsheet, Changing Row Height, Fonts, Bold, Italics, Shade, Grid Lines, Underline, Colors, Landscape Print

RESAVE AS: SALARY

This salary report for the week ending May 30, 1995 will be presented to the vice-president of the company; therefore, it would be a good idea to improve its appearance.

HELPFUL HINTS

➔ You may choose the color of your choice for the background and text. When changing both colors, only highlight once and then make both choices consecutively.

➔ When you change the text and background color, do not choose the same color for both because the text will not be visible.

Directions

1. Retrieve SALARY.
2. Increase the row height of rows 1 and 2 and change the point size to 16.
3. Center the heading across the spreadsheet.
4. Underline the labels in rows 1 and 2.
5. Lightly shade, and change the font on the text in rows 1 and 2.
6. Enter grid lines from A1..J20.
7. Italicize all of the employees names.
8. Bold the entire spreadsheet.
9. Change the background and foreground colors in the range A4..J20. Use colors of your choice. This may not be visible in this book.
10. Change to print in landscape (not visible in this book).
11. RESAVE AS: SALARY.
12. Print.

	A	B	C	D	E	F	G	H	I	J
1					SALARY REPORT					
2					WEEK ENDING MAY 30, 1995					
3										
4	SOCIAL SECURITY		DATE	TOTAL	HOURLY	GROSS				
5	NUMBER	NAME	HIRED	HOURS	RATE	PAY	F.W.T.	S.S.T.	INSURANCE	NET PAY
6										
7	123-78-9087	*THOMPSON, JAMES*	1/14/82	40	$9.25	$370.00	$74.00	$26.53	$44.00	
8	665-65-7654	*HiBBERD, BETSY*	6/5/88	35	$12.65	$442.75	$88.55	$31.75	$44.00	
9	997-89-2343	*POLINOWSKI, SUSAN*	11/12/92	40	$14.75	$590.00	$118.00	$42.30	$44.00	
10	342-76-9981	*ROYCHOUD, ALBERT*	5/17/69	47	$22.67	$1,065.49	$213.10	$76.40	$44.00	
11	357-63-0070	*ALYANAKIAN, LOUIS*	12/19/83	32	$11.55	$369.60	$73.92	$26.50	$44.00	
12	411-12-0700	*GRAILNIK, SHIRLEY*	2/22/94	27	$10.35	$279.45	$55.89	$20.04	$44.00	
13	769-31-5432	*WHEAT, CINDERELLA*	4/29/80	40	$13.95	$558.00	$111.60	$40.01	$44.00	
14	547-76-3211	*SCHER, EVELYN*	4/9/94	30	$15.25	$457.50	$91.50	$32.80	$44.00	
15	231-98-6665	*THOMPSON, CHRIS*	5/23/95	44	$7.75	$341.00	$68.20	$24.45	$44.00	
16	665-01-0041	*GREY, EVELYN*	5/25/95	36	$8.10	$291.60	$58.32	$20.91	$44.00	
17	TOTAL									
18	AVERAGE									
19	LOWEST									
20	HIGHEST									
21										
22	SALARY									
23	EXERCISE 67									

Notes:

Exercise 68 - Shade, Bold, Cell Borders

RESAVE AS: MYBUDGET

You have decided to reformat the spreadsheet MYBUDGET and improve its appearance.

Directions

1. Retrieve MYBUDGET.
2. Format as currency with two decimal places.
3. Format row 34 for whole numbers.
4. Increase the row height, bold, and make the point size 14 in cell A1.
5. Enter a border around cells A1 and also around E1, F1, G1 and H1.
6. Underline each label in column A.
7. Bold and italicize amounts for savings (entire row 38).
8. Shade all values from E12 to H28.
9. Italicize the values in row 30.
10. Enlarge the point in row 36.
11. Shade the range A2..B2.
12. Shade the values in rows 7, 30, 32, 36 and 38.
13. You may also make two changes of your choice.
14. RESAVE AS: MYBUDGET.

	A	B	C	D	E	F	G	H
1	**MONTHLY BUDGET FOR MONTH OF**				**JANUARY**	**FEBRUARY**	**MARCH**	**APRIL**
2	RAISE:	2%						
3	TOTAL INCOME							
4	MONTHLY PAYCHECK				$2,011.00	$2,051.22	$2,092.24	$2,134.09
5	MISCELLANEOUS INCOME				$290.00	$295.80	$301.72	$307.75
6								
7	TOTAL AVAILABLE				$2,301.00	$2,347.02	$2,393.96	$2,441.84
8								
9								
10	TOTAL EXPENSES							
11								
12	MORTGAGE				$475.00	$475.00	$475.00	$475.00
13	CAR PAYMENT				$236.00	$236.00	$236.00	$236.00
14	GAS FOR CAR				$55.00	$55.00	$55.00	$55.00
15	TELEPHONE				$49.00	$85.00	$93.00	$48.00
16	WATER				$39.00	$39.00	$39.00	$39.00
17	SEWAGE				$30.00	$30.00	$30.00	$30.00
18	CABLE				$25.00	$25.00	$25.00	$25.00
19	ELECTRIC				$109.00	$109.00	$109.00	$109.00
20	VISA				$80.00	$80.00	$80.00	$80.00
21	MASTERCARD				$140.00	$140.00	$140.00	$140.00
22	LACY'S				$60.00	$60.00	$60.00	$60.00
23	INSURANCE				$290.00	$290.00	$290.00	$290.00
24	DOCTOR BILLS				$45.00	$45.00	$45.00	$45.00
25	DENTIST BILLS				$0.00	$175.00	$0.00	$0.00
26	WAGE TAX				$22.00	$22.00	$22.00	$22.00
27	INSURANCE				$280.00	$280.00	$280.00	$280.00
28	OTHER				$79.00	$99.00	$167.00	$140.00
29								
30	TOTAL EXPENSES				*$2,014.00*	*$2,245.00*	*$2,146.00*	*$2,074.00*
31								
32	MONTHLY PAYCHECK AFTER EXPENSES				$287.00	$102.02	$247.96	$367.84
33								
34	NUMBER OF DAYS TO NEXT PAYCHECK				11	11	8	11
35								
36	DAILY EXPENSES@20 PER DAY				$220.00	$220.00	$160.00	$220.00
37								
38	***TOTAL AVAILABLE FOR SAVINGS***				***$67.00***	***($117.98)***	***$87.96***	***$147.84***
39								
40								
41	MYBUDGET							
42	EXERCISE 68							

Exercise 69 - Bold, Italics, Row Height, Fonts, Shade, Printing with Gridlines

RESAVE AS: VACATION

Vanessa would like to improve the appearance of this spreadsheet because her boss has asked her for a copy.

HELPFUL HINTS

- In this spreadsheet, be creative in changing its appearance.
- The directions are used as guidelines. You may choose specific row height, fonts and other changes at your discretion.

Directions

1. Retrieve VACATION.
2. Increase the row size and point size of row 1.
3. Italicize and change the color of the text of row 1.
4. Add the values for THREE DAYS.
5. Format all values as currency with no decimal places.
6. Increase the point size and bold the headings in A3 and A13.
7. Darkly shade A5..D5 and A15..D15.
8. Change the background color in A7..A11 and A17..A21.
9. Shade D7..D11 and D17..D21.
10. Make other changes of your choice.
11. RESAVE AS: VACATION.
12. Print with gridlines.

	A	B	C	D
1	***VANESSA'S CRUISE***			
2				
3	**BERMUDA**			
4				
5	ROOMS	ONE DAY	TWO DAYS	THREE DAYS
6				
7	ECONOMY	$489.00	$639.00	$746.00
8	STANDARD	$534.00	$684.00	$801.00
9	DELUXE	$579.00	$729.00	$921.00
10	SUPER	$606.00	$756.00	$945.00
11	MAJESTIC	$640.00	$790.00	$974.00
12				
13	**JAMAICA**			
14				
15	ROOMS	ONE DAY	TWO DAYS	THREE DAYS
16				
17	ECONOMY	$532.00	$732.00	$890.00
18	STANDARD	$587.00	$787.00	$957.00
19	DELUXE	$623.00	$823.00	$1,012.00
20	SUPER	$658.00	$858.00	$1,034.00
21	MAJESTIC	$711.00	$911.00	$1,123.00
22				
23	CRUISE			
24	EXERCISE 69			

Exercise 70 - Centering the Heading across the Spreadsheet, Row Height, Fonts, Borders, Bold, Italics, Color, Shading

RESAVE AS: JEWELRY

Myers Discount Jewelry is doing quite well. You want to improve the appearance of the spreadsheet before giving it to the board of directors.

Directions

1. Retrieve JEWELRY.
2. Do the following to the content of A1 and A2 by only higlighting once: increase the row height, change the point size to 16, change the color of the text, italicize, shade, add a cell border, and center it across the spreadsheet.
3. Create a cell border around cells A6..F7.
4. Shade A6..F7. This may not be visible in this book.
5. Enter cell borders around each cell in the range A9..F19 and A21..F25.
6. Change the point size to 12 for the column headings from A6..F7.
7. Bold the entire spreadsheet.
8. RESAVE AS: JEWELRY.

	A	B	C	D	E	F
1	*MYERS DISCOUNT JEWELRY*					
2	*MERV'S WHOLESALE JEWELRY*					
3						
4	SALES TAX:	8%				
5						
6		COST	MARKUP	SELLING	SALES	TOTAL
7	ITEM	PER ITEM		PRICE	TAX	PRICE
8						
9	ONYX RING	$99	240%			
10	DIAMOND BRACELET	$290	600%			
11	SWISS WATCH	$240	425%			
12	RUBY TIARA	$400	700%			
13	GOLD ROPE CHAIN	$200	425%			
14	TURQUOISE RING	$190	490%			
15	EMERALD WATCH	$359	600%			
16	PEARL BRACELET	$202	250%			
17	OPAL RING	$349	350%			
18	ONYX BRACELET	$130	200%			
19	RUBY NECKLACE	$500	390%			
20						
21	TOTAL					
22	AVERAGE					
23	LOWEST					
24	HIGHEST					
25	NUMBER OF ITEMS					
26						
27	JEWELRY					
28	EXERCISE 70					

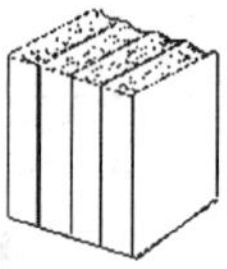

Exercise 71 - Concepts Summary Exercise

SAVE AS: BOOKS

The owner of the Read Me Book Store would like to compare the total value of the present stock to the total value of the new stock that will be added.

Directions

1. Create a spreadsheet with the following information.

TYPE	PRESENT STOCK	VALUE OF EACH	NEW STOCK	VALUE OF EACH
NOVELS	670	6.50	290	7.89
TRAVEL	288	8.85	356	11.25
COMPUTERS	354	20.21	403	24.50
BUSINESS	890	5.75	798	10.90
EDUCATION	766	12.89	598	11.45
PHOTOGRAPHY	560	34.76	460	33.75
NUTRITION	660	22.19	640	23.19
COOKING	750	12.50	620	10.25
SEWING	230	9.90	350	11.68
SPORTS	990	17.89	960	25..95

2. Create a formula to compute the following:
   TOTAL VALUE (each) for the present stock. Hint: Use present stock x value.
   TOTAL VALUE for the new stock.
   INCREASE or the DECREASE of the total value from the present stock to the new stock. Was there an increase or decrease in the Total stock from present stock to new stock? What was the Total increase or decrease?
   TOTAL *present* stock and *new* stock.
   AVERAGES for *present* stock, *new* stock, and increase or decrease.
3. Increase the row height, add shading, bold, italicize, add text and background color, change fonts and increase or decrease point size to your discretion.
4. SAVE AS: BOOKS. Print in landscape with gridlines.

	A	B	C	D	E	F	G	H
1								
2								
3								
4								
5								
6								
7								
8								
9								
10								
11								
12								
13								
14								
15								
16								
17								
18								
19								
20								
21								
22								
23								
24								
25								
26								
27								

Exercise 72 - Concepts Summary Exercise

SAVE AS: CLASTRIP

The juniors and seniors of Center Township High School in Monaca, PA will be taking a class trip to Washington, D.C. They will be having fund-raisers to raise money for this trip and they would like to know the Total cost of the trip for each student based on the Total Bus Fare, Hotel, and Fees for the entire trip after the money raised from the fund raisers has been deducted.

Directions

1. Input the following information directly into the computer.
2. The Bus Fare for each student is $55.55; the Hotel is $59.95; the Fees are a total of $286.50 and Miscellaneous expenses are $190.
3. Create formulas for TOTAL expense for each student.
4. The junior class has had three fund-raisers and they have raised the following amounts: first fund-raiser, they raised $900; the second fund-raiser, they raised $1400; and the third fund-raiser, they raised $1100.
5. The senior class had two fund-raisers and have raised the following amounts: the first fund-raiser, they raised $1600 and the second fund-raiser, they raised $1300.
6. Enter a formula to add the TOTAL amounts raised by each class.
7. Enter another formula to show how the TOTAL expenses will be decreased for each junior and senior by evenly dividing the proceeds from the fund-raisers.
8. Increase the size of rows and enlarge their fonts, bold, italicize, shade, etc. at your discretion.
9. SAVE AS: CLASTRIP.
10. Print in landscape with gridlines.

STUDENTS' NAME	*GRADE*	*STUDENTS' NAME*	*GRADE*
HERSH, CHARLES	SENIOR	RAYMOND, DAVE	JUNIOR
MORRIS, STEVE	SENIOR	BARNABY, FRED	JUNIOR
POPE, SANDRA	SENIOR	HEFELFINGER, JIM	JUNIOR
RYMER, MELISSA	SENIOR	ANDERS, SUSAN	JUNIOR
COBBS, ROSHAWNA	SENIOR	HARRIS, YVONNE	JUNIOR
MOSEL, ADAM	SENIOR	MORELLA, ROBIN	JUNIOR
CLARKE, JENNIFER	SENIOR	CHUN, KI PUNG	JUNIOR
JOHNSON, ERIC	SENIOR	GEIBER, ANDREA	JUNIOR
MASON, PAM	SENIOR	LAMBERT, ROSE	JUNIOR
GINGRICH, LINDA	SENIOR	MOROSA, ARLENE	JUNIOR
MOFFETT, MANDY	SENIOR	BRIDWELL,JAYNE	JUNIOR
MANCINI, ELYSE KARA	SENIOR	CHU, LU	JUNIOR
JONES, DWAYNE	SENIOR	CHANG, THERESA	JUNIOR
PLUM, KRISTA	SENIOR	JONES, JAMAL	JUNIOR
IRVONETTI, LYNETTE	SENIOR	BUSIN, ED	JUNIOR

Competencies:

After completing this unit, you will know how to:

1. Change the model's appearance by using WYSIWYG
2. Bold
3. Underline
4. Shade
5. Italics
6. Change row height
7. Enter cell border
8. Enter a border outline around a range
9. Change colors
10. Print in landscape

UNIT 9

Concepts:

Headers and Footers
Printing Multiple Copies
Setting and Clearing a Print Range
Printing with Gridlines
Printing a Selected Range
Page Breaks and Page Numbering
Moving (Cutting and Pasting) and Windows
Compressed Print
Naming Ranges

Points to Remember:

- Most print commands are set through the print setting or page setup screens.
- Headers print on the top of every page of a larger spreadsheet and they can contain dates, text, or cell references.
- Footers print on the bottom of every page and can contain the same types of information as a header.
- Formatting changes (bold, font, etc.) can be applied to headers and footers.
- Check the print preview screen before printing.
- Most software programs allow *custom* headers and footers.
- Compressed print and landscape are very useful for large spreadsheets.
- When naming a range, choose a name relevant to the data.
- Headers and footers are not visible in this unit of the book.
- *From this point on in the book, grids are not provided in the Concepts Summary exercises. Spreadsheets will be directly entered into the computer. An optional grid is available for copying at the end of the book.*

Exercise 73 - Header, Footer, Printing Multiple Copies, Landscape, Gridlines, Compressed Print

RESAVE AS: EXPENSES

Sweets Candy Company is ready to print a report of its expenses but the increase rate will be changed from 6.25% to 8.25%. When this is changed, every value in the spreadsheet will change to adjust to the absolute value.

HELPFUL HINTS

➔ Landscape print will print the spreadsheet horizontally on the page.
➔ A header prints on the top of every page and a footer prints on the bottom of every page.
➔ When changing the annual increase rate, check the values and make sure they automatically adjust to reflect the change.

Directions

1. Retrieve EXPENSES.
2. Change the annual increase rate in cell B4 to 8.25%. Each formula will automatically recalculate.
3. Increase the row height, the point size, and change the font of all of the cells in the entire spreadsheet.
4. Create the Header:
   Eight Year Report (right justify)
5. Create the Footer:
   The current date (centered).
6. RESAVE AS: EXPENSES.
7. Set to print for two copies through the print setting screen.
8. Print in landscape with gridlines in compressed print to fit on one page.

	A	B	C	D
1	PROJECTION OF BUSINESS EXPENSES			
2	SWEETS CANDY COMPANY			
3				
4	ANNUAL INCREASE RATE:	8.25%		
5				
6	EXPENSES	YEAR 1	YEAR 2	YEAR 3
7				
8	RENT	$14,567.00		
9	UTILITIES	$1,198.00		
10	MACHINERY UPKEEP	$1,010.00		
11	SALARIES	$387,000.00		
12	ADVERTISING	$8,235.00		
13	DELIVERY/FREIGHT	$1,500.00		
14				
15	TOTAL	$413,510.00		
16				
17	EXPENSES			
18	EXERCISE 73			

	E	F	G	H	I
1					
2					
3					
4					
5					
6	YEAR 4	YEAR 5	YEAR 6	YEAR 7	YEAR 8
7					
8					
9					
10					
11					
12					
13					
14					
15					
16					
17					
18					

Exercise 74 - Header, Footer, Setting and Clearing the Print Range

RESAVE AS: SALARY

The Salary Report needs to include only the social security numbers, employees' names, date hired, total hours, hourly rate, gross pay, and totals of each.

HELPFUL HINTS

- ➔ There are two ways to print the selected range: highlighting the print range or setting the range as an absolute value.
- ➔ You do not need to print rows 18, 19 or 20 for this report.

Directions

1. Retrieve SALARY.
2. Create a Header:
   Pay Report (right justify).
3. Create a footer:
   Week Ending May 30, 1995 (centered).
4. Set the print range of A1..F17.
5. Add grid lines from A1..F17.
6. Adjust the horizontal centering of the heading in the first two rows to center across column A to column F.
7. Print only that selected area (A1..F17).
8. Clear the print range.
9. RESAVE AS: SALARY.

SALARY REPORT WEEK ENDING MAY 30, 1995					
SOCIAL SECURITY NUMBER	NAME	DATE HIRED	TOTAL HOURS	HOURLY RATE	GROSS PAY
123-78-9087	*THOMPSON, JAMES*	1/14/82	40	$9.25	$370.00
665-65-7654	*HIBBERD, BETSY*	6/5/88	35	$12.65	$442.75
997-89-2343	*POLINOWSKI, SUSAN*	11/12/92	40	$14.75	$590.00
342-76-9981	*ROYCHOUD, ALBERT*	5/17/69	47	$22.67	$1,065.49
357-63-0070	*ALYANAKIAN, LOUIS*	12/19/83	32	$11.55	$369.60
411-12-0700	*GRAILNIK, SHIRLEY*	2/22/94	27	$10.35	$279.45
769-31-5432	*WHEAT, CINDERELLA*	4/29/80	40	$13.95	$558.00
547-76-3211	*SCHER, EVELYN*	4/9/94	30	$15.25	$457.50
231-98-6665	*THOMPSON, CHRIS*	5/23/95	44	$7.75	$341.00
665-01-0041	*GREY, EVELYN*	5/25/95	36	$8.10	$291.60
TOTAL			371	$126.27	$4,765.39

Notes:

Exercise 75 - Inserting, Moving (Cutting and Pasting), Windows, Header, Footer, Printing Selected Ranges, Landscape, Compressed

RESAVE AS: ENGLISH

Miss Tia Cheer has decided to give her English class an extra test at the end of the term. She also has decided to add a homework grade.

Directions

1. Retrieve ENGLISH.
2. Insert a blank column E for TEST 4 scores, type TEST 4 in cell E4, and HOMEWORK in cell J4.
3. Type the word AVERAGE in cell K4. This is the *final grade* AVERAGE - not a test or spelling average.
4. Create a vertical window in column B so the students' names will remain visible.
5. Enter the TEST 4 scores in column E and HOMEWORK grades in column J.
6. Check all your formulas and make sure they have all adjusted.
7. To compute the AVERAGE final grade in column K, Miss Cher counts the test *average* as 65%, the spelling *average* as 20% and homework grade as 15%.
8. Enter the formula for AVERAGE in K6 and copy down. Clear the window.
9. SAVE AS: ENGLISH and print in compressed and landscape.

	A	B	C	D	E	F	G	H	I	J	K
1	MISS TIA CHER										
2	ENGLISH										
3											
4		TEST 1	TEST 2	TEST 3	TEST 4	TEST AVG.	SPEL 1	SPEL 2	SPELLING AVG.	HOMEWORK	AVERAGE
5											
6	ANDERS, ROBERT	97	95	91	96		88	96		91	
7	BROTHERSTON, JOHN	97	100	97	99		100	100		100	
8	BENJAMIN, MARIE	91	90	100	90		96	96		95	
9	CLEVELAND, ELYSE	94	100	95	92		96	88		89	
10	CRONIN, KURT	100	100	100	95		72	100		76	
11	WHITBY, SUSAN	97	95	100	98		100	100		94	
12	DAVIS, SARAH	100	100	100	91		100	100		100	
13	HARRISON, BARBARA	97	100	100	84		96	96		99	
14	McFERSON, CONNIE	82	85	0	71		80	88		80	
15	MITCHELL, DAVID	81	95	100	82		84	92		90	
16	PERICELLI, ANTHONY	80	100	100	93		96	100		82	
17	RICHARDSON, LESLIE	97	100	100	91		72	96		70	
18	SANTINI, MICHAEL	70	75	93	62		60	88		97	
19	ZIMMERS, WILLIAM	91	95	96	84		96	100		98	
20											
21	ENGLISH										
22	EXERCISE 75										

10. Go to column B and insert a blank column.
11. Move (cut and paste) the AVERAGES from column K to column B. The formulas should automatically adjust.
12. Create a Header:
    Current date (right justified).
15. Create a Footer:
    English Averages (left justified), Semester 2 (centered) and your name (right justified).
16. Make changes at your discretion in the fonts, point size, bold, italics, etc.
17. Insert a blank row after each students' name.
18. Select the print range as A1..B35 which will include only the students' names and their grades (AVERAGE final grade).
19. SAVE AS: ENGLISH.
20. Print the selected range with student names and AVERAGES – from A1 to B35.

	A	B
1	*MISS TIA CHER*	
2	*ENGLISH*	
3		
4		*AVERAGE*
5		
6	*ANDERS, ROBERT*	
7		
8	*BROTHERSTON, JOHN*	
9		
10	*BENJAMIN, MARIE*	
11		
12	*CLEVELAND, ELYSE*	
13		
14	*CRONIN, KURT*	
15		
16	*WHITBY, SUSAN*	
17		
18	*DAVIS, SARAH*	
19		
20	*HARRISON, BARBARA*	
21		
22	*McFERSON, CONNIE*	
23		
24	*MITCHELL, DAVID*	
25		
26	*PERICELLI, ANTHONY*	
27		
28	*RICHARDSON, LESLIE*	
29		
30	*SANTINI, MICHAEL*	
31		
32	*ZIMMERS, WILLIAM*	
33		
34	*ENGLISH*	
35	*EXERCISE 75*	

Exercise 76 - Inserting, Copying a Template, Header, Footer, Page Break

RESAVE AS: GRADES

Krista Beaumont has computed her first semester grades and is now ready to compute her second semester grades. She will copy the entire model (the template) and change all the grades from Semester 1 as indicated for Semester 2. (The model contains values, labels and formulas and the template removes or changes values, while leaving the labels and formulas.)

Her second semester grades will automatically calculate every time she *enters* a new value. She also would like each semester printed on a separate page.

Directions

1. Retrieve GRADES.
2. Erase A19 and A20.
3. Insert a blank row 3.
4. Type SEMESTER 1 in A3.
5. Copy the entire model from A1..F17 to A22..F38.
6. Change Semester 1 to Semester 2 in A24.
7. Type the test scores for Semester 2 over the test scores for Semester 1.
   HINT: Do not delete the cell contents and then enter Semester 2 – use overtype.
8. The template (model) should automatically compute the TEST AVERAGE in column F for Semester 2 as each new grade is entered.
9. Format column F for numbers with 1 decimal place.
10. Create the following Header:
    Semester Grades—Junior Year, 1995 (right justified).
11. Create the following Footer:
    Krista Beaumont (left justified) and page number (right justified).
12. Enter a page break to print Semester 1 on page 1 and Semester 2 on page 2.
13. RESAVE AS: GRADES.
14. Print Semester 1 and Semester 2 on separate pages.

	A	B	C	D	E	F
1	FIRST SEMESTER GRADES					
2	JUNIOR YEAR -- 1995					
3	SEMESTER 1					
4						
5	COURSE	TEST 1	TEST 2	TEST 3	TEST 4	TEST AVERAGE
6						
7	ENGLISH	98	100	91	88	94.3
8						
9	HISTORY	92	90	87	86	88.8
10						
11	SPANISH	97	85	89	90	90.3
12						
13	PHYSICS	99	98	100	100	99.3
14						
15	CALCULUS	100	90	95	91	94.0
16						
17	PSYCHOLOGY	85	87	100	100	93.0
18						
19						
20						
21						
22	SECOND SEMESTER GRADES					
23	JUNIOR YEAR -- 1995					
24	SEMESTER 2					
25						
26	COURSE	TEST 1	TEST 2	TEST 3	TEST 4	TEST AVERAGE
27						
28	ENGLISH	97	89	96	91	93.3
29						
30	HISTORY	88	87	80	76	82.8
31						
32	SPANISH	100	90	98	99	96.8
33						
34	PHYSICS	100	83	72	99	88.5
35						
36	CALCULUS	96	81	88	100	91.3
37						
38	PSYCHOLOGY	100	99	99	100	99.5
39						
40						
41	GRADES					
42	EXERCISE 76					

Exercise 77 - Naming Ranges, Header, Footer, Page Numbering, Compressed Print

RESAVE AS: WEDDING

Michael and Vanessa would like each restaurant's estimate for their wedding reception on separate pages.

Directions

1. Retrieve WEDDING.
2. Create a range name for all of the information about the MONT CHATEAU RESTAURANT–from A7..F17. The range name is CHATEAU.
3. Create a range name for all of the information about the WALLINGFORD INN–from A18..F28. The range name is WALLING.
4. Create a range name for all of the information about the ROMEO and JULIET CASTLE INN–from A29..F40. The range name is CASTLE.
5. Create a Header:
   Reception Arrangements (left) and current date (right).
6. Create a Footer:
   MICHAEL AND VANESSA'S WEDDING (left) and page number (right).
6. RESAVE AS WEDDING.
7. Print in compressed print on three separate pages by range names.

	A	B	C	D	E	F
1		MICHAEL AND VANESSA'S WEDDING				
2		RECEPTION ARRANGEMENTS				
3						
4	AMOUNT OF GUESTS			100		
5						
6						
7	MONT CHATEAU RESTAURANT					
8						
9	RECEPTION	MEAL	TOTAL MEAL COST	HORS D'OERVES	TOTAL	MEAL AND
10	MENU	PER PERSON	OF ALL GUESTS	PER PERSON	HORS D'OERVES	HORS D'OERVES
11						
12	CHICKEN DIANE	$42.50	$4,250.00	$7.50	$750.00	$5,000.00
13	SIRLOIN TIPS	$47.50	$4,750.00	$8.00	$800.00	$5,550.00
14	PORK CHOPS	$55.00	$5,500.00	$8.50	$850.00	$6,350.00
15	SURF/TURF	$66.75	$6,675.00	$9.50	$950.00	$7,625.00
16						
17						
18	WALLINGFORD INN					
19						
20	RECEPTION	MEAL	TOTAL MEAL COST	HORS D'OERVES	TOTAL	MEAL AND
21	MENU	PER PERSON	OF ALL GUESTS	PER PERSON	HORS D'OERVES	HORS D'OERVES
22						
23	CHICKEN DIANE	$46.75	$4,675.00	$6.30	$630.00	$5,305.00
24	SIRLOIN TIPS	$49.00	$4,900.00	$7.00	$700.00	$5,600.00
25	PORK CHOPS	$54.50	$5,450.00	$7.50	$750.00	$6,200.00
26	SURF/TURF	$68.75	$6,875.00	$8.25	$825.00	$7,700.00
27						
28						
29	ROMEO AND JULIET CASTLE INN					
30						
31	RECEPTION	MEAL	TOTAL MEAL COST	HORS D'OERVES	TOTAL	MEAL AND
32	MENU	PER PERSON	OF ALL GUESTS	PER PERSON	HORS D'OERVES	HORS D'OERVES
33						
34	CHICKEN DIANE	$50.50	$5,050.00	$7.25	$725.00	$5,775.00
35	SIRLOIN TIPS	$53.60	$5,360.00	$7.75	$775.00	$6,135.00
36	PORK CHOPS	$57.75	$5,775.00	$8.65	$865.00	$6,640.00
37	SURF/TURF	$73.50	$7,350.00	$9.25	$925.00	$8,275.00
38						
39	WEDDING					
40	EXERCISE 77					

Exercise 78 - Concepts Summary Exercise

SAVE AS: COOLIT

Coolit Air Conditioning Company is owned by two brothers, Joseph A. J. Mancini and Flavion S. Mancini. This spreadsheet is a statement of Projected Sales for 1997 for the *Coolit Company*.

Based on the performance of several past years' sales, second quarter sales generally increase by several percent over first quarter sales.

Directions

1. Create a spreadsheet for the Coolit Air Conditioning Company:

PROJECTED SALES -- 1997					
COOL-IT AIR CONDITIONING					
QUARTERLY REPORT					
FIRST QUARTER SALES					
	NORTHEAST	SOUTHEAST	CENTRAL	NORTHWEST	SOUTHWEST
JANUARY	$189,000	$233,000	$151,951	$456,700	$356,760
FEBRUARY	$196,870	$247,000	$162,321	$538,900	$342,567
MARCH	$355,990	$237,900	$163,567	$765,980	$431,190
TOTAL					

2. Enter a formula to compute Total Sales for the Northeast, Southeast, etc.
3. Below the Total Sales, enter SECOND QUARTER SALES.
4. Enter the months (April, May, June) and copy the areas (Northeast, etc.).
5. The sales from March to April increase in each area as follows: Northeast increases by 7% each month; Southeast increases by 5%; Central increases by 2%; Northwest increases by 7%; and the Southwest increases by 4%.
6. Enter a formula in the Northeast column to show the increase from March to April.
7. Enter a formula for May. HINT: This increases 7% per month in the second quarter so the 7% in May will compute from April. Copy the formula for June Sales. *Be careful when copying this formula.*

8. Enter a formula for April to increase 5% from March for the Southeast. It increases 5% every month in the second quarter. *Be careful when copying.*
9. Continue entering formulas for Central, Northwest, and the Southwest.
10. Enter a formula for Total Sales for the second quarter.
11. Create a Header of your choice and a Footer of your choice.
12. SAVE AS: COOLIT.
13. Bold the area that had the highest sales in the *first* quarter.
14. Bold the area that had the highest sales in the *second* quarter.
15. Print quarters on separate pages.

Exercise 79 - Concepts Summary Exercise

SAVE AS: MACHINE

This spreadsheet will show depreciation of *Machine X* and *Machine Z.* Calculate the depreciation of *Machine X* for five years and *Machine Z* for seven years. Machine X was purchased for $15,000. The cost of the machine, salvage value, and number of total years are used to compute the depreciation for each of the 5 years and the ending book value for each of the five years. The ending book value equals value after depreciation.

Directions

1. Enter the following information in a spreadsheet.

MACHINE X

Cost of Machine X	$15,000	
Salvage Value	$5,000	
Number of Total Years	5	
YEAR	DEPRECIATION	ENDING BOOK VALUE
0	0	$15,000
1		
2		
3		
4		
5		

2. All formulas in the *Depreciation* column must be *absolute* formulas. In the depreciation column for Year 1 the formula is the (*Cost of the Machine – Salvage Value) /the Number of Total Years*. All three cell addresses are absolute – use parentheses.

3. Copy the formula down the depreciation column. The depreciation should be the same *each* year.
4. The Ending Book Value formula is *not* an absolute formula. To compute Ending Book Value, subtract the Depreciation of Year 1 from the Ending Book Value Year 0.
5. Copy the formula down.
6. Now you are ready to compute depreciation and book value for Machine Z.

Cost of Machine Z $22,000
Salvage Value: $7,000
Number of Total Years: 7

YEAR	DEPRECIATION	ENDING BOOK VALUE
0	0	$22,000
1		
2		
3		
4		
5		
6		
7		

7. Copy the template from Machine X and change the labels and the values for the cost of Machine Z, salvage value and number of years.
8. Create a Header:
   Depreciation Statements –Machine X and Machine Z.(left).
9. Create a Footer:
   Current Date (left) and your name (right).
10. SAVE AS: MACHINE.
11. Print Machine X and Machine Z on two separate pages with gridlines.

Competencies:

After completing this unit, you will know how to:

1. Enter and print headers and footers
2. Print multiple copies
3. Clear a print range
4. Create and copy a template
5. Print with gridlines
6. Print a selected range
7. Enter page breaks
8. Enter page numbers
9. Use windows to split the screen
10. Move (cut and paste) information
11. Print with compressed text
12. Name ranges

UNIT 10

Concepts:

"If" Statements
"Date" Functions
Splitting the Screen (Freeze)
Windows
Advanced Formulas with Percents
Inserting
Creating and Copying a Template Range
"PMT" Statement
Global Settings

Points to Remember:

- Functions have a specific structure you must follow. Every function must include a function name–usually a contraction of the full name.
- Never include a space in a function.
- "If" statements are extremely useful in many electronic spreadsheets used in business because they allow the computer to make use of its decision making capabilities.
- There are three parts to an "If" statement. The first part is the condition; the second part is what the computer performs if the condition is true; the third part is what the computer performs if the condition is false.
- "PMT" statements can be used to calculate most loans including home equity, car, etc.
- "Date" functions enter dates as values that can calculate.
- Global settings affect the entire spreadsheet while range commands affect only the range you are working on.

Exercise 80 -"If" Statements, Bold, Italics, Fonts, Landscape, Gridlines

RESAVE AS: COMMISS

Calderi's Real Estate has decided to give a $1000 bonus to salespersons who have sold more than $600,000. If they have sold less than $600,000, they will receive no bonus. They would also like to include types of areas, such as *rural* or *suburban,* on this spreadsheet.

HELPFUL HINTS

- ➔ An "If" statement allows the computer to use decision making capabilities.
- ➔ "If" statements contain three parts: part one is the condition; part two is what the computer performs if the condition is true; part three is what the computer performs if the condition is false.
- ➔ Use relational operators (= equal, > greater than, < less than, etc.) in the condition.

Directions

1. Retrieve COMMISS.
2. Enter the information in H6, I5 and I6 as shown.
3. In cell H8, create an "If" statement showing that If the agents SALES are $600,000 or more they will receive a $1000 BONUS. If their sales are less than $600,000, they will not receive a BONUS (put 0 in the cell).
4. Copy the formula from H8 to H9..H15.
5. In cell I8, enter another "If" statement. This statement will use column B to build its condition. "If" the LOCATION in column B is THORNBURY, put the word Suburban in the cell. If the AREA is not THORNBURY, put the word Rural in I8.
6. Copy the formula down from I8 to I9..I15.
7. Bold and italicize all column headings, increase the size of the labels in rows 1, 2, and 3 and enter a border around this heading.
8. RESAVE AS: COMMISS.
9. Print in landscape with gridlines.

	A	B	C	D	E	F	G	H	I
1	*CALDERI'S REAL ESTATE*								
2	*COMMISSION REPORT*								
3	*WEEK ENDING MAY 30, 1996*								
4									
5				***COMM.***		***BASE***	***TOTAL***		***RURAL OR***
6	***AGENT***	***LOCATION***	***SALES***	***RATE***	***COMMISSION***	***SALARY***	***SALARY***	***BONUS***	***SUBURBAN***
7									
8	LOCKWOOD	LOGANWOOD	$987,000	6%	$59,220	$1,500	$60,720		
9	DEADY	THORNBURY	$634,000	6%	$38,040	$1,500	$39,540		
10	BELSASCO	PINEHURST	$854,000	6%	$51,240	$1,500	$52,740		
11	SOSTMANN	WILLOUGHBY	$550,000	6%	$33,000	$1,500	$34,500		
12	POWELL	LOGANWOOD	$654,000	6%	$39,240	$1,500	$40,740		
13	WHITMORE	PINEHURST	$439,000	6%	$26,340	$1,500	$27,840		
14	SONG	MONACO	$689,000	6%	$41,340	$1,500	$42,840		
15	COAKLEY	THORNBURY	$320,000	6%	$19,200	$1,500	$20,700		
16									
17	TOTAL				$307,620	$12,000	$319,620		
18	AVERAGE								
19	MINIMUM								
20	MAXIMUM								
21									
22	COMMISS								
23	EXERCISE 80								

Notes:

Exercise 81 - Inserting, "If" Statements, "Date" Functions, Window

RESAVE AS: DOCTOR

A few patients need to be added to the original list and the doctor needs to determine which patients still have an unpaid balance.

Directions

1. Retrieve DOCTOR.
2. Erase the cells C7..C13 as a range. Re-enter dates as "Date" Functions. (Dates entered as Date Functions are entered as values.) Enter them in C7 through C13. Delete row 16.
3. Insert a blank row after each patient's name.
4. Add the new patients and new information to the spreadsheet as shown.
5. Copy the formula down column F to compute amount owed for each new patient entered. Delete the zeros in the blank rows.
6. Create a vertical window in column B before entering the following information.
7. In G7, create an "If" statement. If the patient has a zero balance, put PAID in the cell. If the patient has a balance, put OVERDUE in the cell. Copy the formula down column G and delete any zeros in cells.
8. In column H, create another "If" statement that would set a condition based on the age column. If a patient's age is 62 or over, YES they have Medicare. If they are under 62, NO.
9. In row 35, enter a formula for TOTAL of DUE, PAID, and AMOUNT OWED and in row 36 compute AVERAGES for DUE, PAID and AMOUNT OWED.
10. Format columns D, E, and F as currency with no decimals.
11. Format the patients' names to center align as a range.
12. Clear the window.
13. RESAVE AS: DOCTOR.
14. Print.

	A	B	C	D	E	F	G	H
1			DR. ANNA STESIA					
2			PATIENT REPORT--1994					
3			WEEK ENDING OCTOBER 17, 1994					
4								
5	PATIENT	AGE	DATE EXAMINED	DUE	PAID	AMOUNT OWED	OVERDUE	MEDICARE
6								
7	O'SULLIVAN, AMY	24	11-Oct-94	$127	$127	$0		
8								
9	ROTHERFORD, MARY	56	11-Oct-94	$78	$50	$28		
10								
11	HIGGINS, JAMES	43	13-Oct-94	$219	$0	$219		
12								
13	BROTHERSTON, FRED	77	13-Oct-94	$45	$45	$0		
14								
15	MEDINA, JOSE	42	14-Oct-94	$45	$20	$25		
16								
17	CALLAGHAN, SUSAN	37	14-Oct-94	$90	$70	$20		
18								
19	CELLINI, ANTHONY	64	15-Oct-94	$137	$27	$110		
20								
21	ALBERTSON, JEN	87	22-Oct-94	$330	$200	$130		
22								
23	LONG, KATIE	69	24-Oct-94	$70	$70	$0		
24								
25	JOHNSON, BILL	32	01-Nov-94	$110	$60	$50		
26								
27	WARD, PAULETTE	46	01-Nov-94	$90	$90	$0		
28								
29	CLARK, DIANE	90	01-Nov-94	$120	$90	$30		
30								
31	KRAMER, ALBERT	39	01-Nov-94	$50	$50	$0		
32								
33	WADDINGTON, BETH	55	03-Nov-94	$90	$90	$0		
34								
35	TOTAL							
36	AVERAGE							
37								
38	DOCTOR							
39	EXERCISE 81							

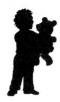

Exercise 82 - Vertical Split, “Date” Function, Printing a Selected Range, “If” Statement

SAVE AS: DOLLS

Cupie has been collecting dolls for years and she has all the original boxes and receipts which helps to retain their value. She was curious as to the percent of increase or decrease in their value over the years.

HELPFUL HINTS

- ➔ Usc thc “Datc” function in column D.
- ➔ To find the percent of the increase or decrease, divide the increase or the decrease by the value at purchase.
- ➔ When splitting the screen (titles) or using windows horizontally, put your cell pointer below the titles you want to see; when splitting vertically, put the cell pointer one column to the right.

Directions

1. Enter the information from the following spreadsheet in columns A, B, C, D (enter as Date function) and E as shown.
2. Vertically split column B to add information in columns F, G, H, and I.
3. Format all labels to center align.
4. Put a formula in cell G6 to find the INCREASE or DECREASE in VALUE.
5. Copy the formula from G6 into G7..G19.
6. Put a formula in cell H6 to compute the PERCENT of the INCREASE or DECREASE.
7. Copy the formula from cell H6 into H7..H19.
8. Format the values in column H as percent with no decimal.

9. Cupie's dolls will be taxed at different rates depending on their increase or decrease of value. Create an If statement in I6 to show if the percent of the increase or decrease is over 20%, compute 5% of the present value. If the increase or decrease is not over 20%, the doll is taxed at 2% of the present value.
10. Copy the formula down column I.
11. Enter a function in cell E21 to find the Total and copy to F21 and G21.
12. Format all values in columns E, F, and G as currency with no decimal.
13. Clear the vertical split.
14. Create a Header and Footer of your choice.
15. SAVE AS: DOLLS.
16. Print the spreadsheet in landscape. Print again but *only* columns A, B, C.

	A	B	C	D	E	F	G	H	I
1	CUPIE GERBER'S DOLL COLLECTION								
2									
3			SPECIAL	DATE	VALUE AT	PRESENT	INC./DEC.	PERCENT	
4	BRAND	DOLL	FEATURES	BOUGHT	PURCHASE	VALUE	VALUE	INC./DEC.	TAX
5									
6	MADAM SANDRA	JULIETTE	ALL LACE	Feb-81	$32	$96			
7	DIMPLES, INC.	JOHN F. KENNEDY	PORCELAIN	Sep-70	$23	$125			
8	MADAM SANDRA	CLEOPATRA	DIAMONDS	Jul-92	$45	$72			
9	MADAM SANDRA	ROMEO	SILK SHIRT	Mar-69	$25	$87			
10	BETTY'S BABIES	SHIRLEY TEMPLE	HUMAN HAIR	Jan-65	$62	$165			
11	BETTY'S BABIES	JUDY GARLAND	OPEN MOUTH	Jun-63	$40	$155			
12	MADAM SANDRA	NAPOLEON	BENDABLE	May-90	$55	$61			
13	MADAM SANDRA	JOSEPHINE	HUMAN HAIR	May-90	$42	$47			
14	DIMPLES, INC.	MARILYN MONROE	PORCELAIN	May-70	$32	$113			
15	BETTY'S BABIES	NEWBORN TWINS	BENDABLE	Nov-83	$65	$47			
16	DIMPLES, INC.	CARY GRANT	SILK SUIT	Jun-63	$41	$111			
17	MADAM SANDRA	QUEEN ELIZABETH	DIAMONDS	Aug-94	$50	$90			
18	BETTY'S BABIES	SPANKY	OPEN MOUTH	Apr-80	$78	$145			
19	DIMPLES, INC.	SANDRA LEE	LACE	May-70	$82	$44			
20									
21	TOTAL								
22									
23	DOLLS								
24	EXERCISE 82								

Notes:

Exercise 83 - Inserting, Formulas with Percents, Page Breaks, Header and Footer

RESAVE AS: SHOTS

The Norcross Basketball Team would like to insert two columns in their report to compute the percent of basketball shots made as well as a column for percent of foul shots made. This would give the coach a better idea of each player's ability.

Directions

1. Retrieve SHOTS.
2. Delete the formulas in F13, F21, F29, and F37.
3. Erase A13, A21, A29 and A37 and enter new information as shown.
4. Enter a function to average the TOTAL POINTS in F13.
5. Copy from F13 to F21, F29 and F37.
6. Insert a blank column D and enter the heading PERCENT MADE as indicated.
7. Enter a formula into D8 to compute percent of *shots* made.
8. Copy the formula down column D into the appropriate cells.
9. Enter a function in D13 to show Average Percent of shots made.
10. Copy from D13 to D21, D29, and D37.
11. Format column D as percent with no decimal places.
12. Also insert a blank column G and enter the heading as indicated.
13. Enter a formula into G8 to compute percent of foul shots made.
14. Copy the formula down column G into the appropriate cells.
15. Enter a function in G13 to show Average Percent Made of *foul* shots.
16. Copy the formula from G13 to G21, G29 and G37.
17. Enter the Header: Your name (right).
18. Enter the Footer: Preliminary Report (left) and today's date (right).
19. Enter a page break between each player.
20. SAVE AS: SHOTS
21. Print. This will print on four separate pages.

	A	B	C	D	E	F	G	H
1	NORCROSS BASKETBALL RECORDS							
2	PRELIMINARY REPORT							
3								
4		SHOTS	SHOTS	PERCENT	FOUL SHOTS	FOUL SHOTS	PERCENT	TOTAL
5	PLAYER	ATTEMPTED	MADE	MADE	ATTEMPTED	MADE	MADE	POINTS
6								
7	ADAMAK, JOHN							
8	GAME 1	17	7		4	4		
9	GAME 2	11	9		2	1		
10	GAME 3	14	6		3	1		
11	GAME 4	9	6		4	0		
12	GAME 5	9	4		2	1		
13	5 GAME AVERAGE							
14								
15	MOLESKY, BRAD							
16	GAME 1	11	8		2	2		
17	GAME 2	9	6		4	0		
18	GAME 3	6	0		2	0		
19	GAME 4	3	3		1	1		
20	GAME 5	4	2		2	1		
21	5 GAME AVERAGE							
22								
23	MARTIN, JONATHAN							
24	GAME 1	8	7		6	3		
25	GAME 2	7	5		4	2		
26	GAME 3	7	1		0	0		
27	GAME 4	9	2		2	1		
28	GAME 5	11	5		2	0		
29	5 GAME AVERAGE							
30								
31	SMITH, DARREN							
32	GAME 1	14	8		1	0		
33	GAME 2	11	3		2	0		
34	GAME 3	9	6		4	2		
35	GAME 4	5	4		4	0		
36	GAME 5	8	1		2	1		
37	5 GAME AVERAGE							
38								
39	SHOTS							
40	EXERCISE 83							

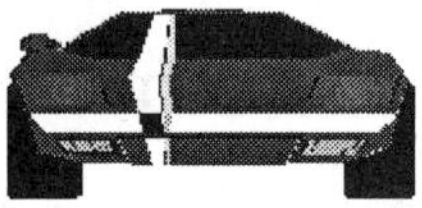

Exercise 84 - Creating a Template for "PMT" Statements, Cell Reference

SAVE AS: AUTO

Because Michael and Vanessa need to start looking for a new car, they want to get an idea of their available cash. Their monthly payments must be conservative. They want to create a template to show available cash and the monthly payments. They were recently in a car accident; therefore, they will receive insurance money.

HELPFUL HINTS

- ➔ A cell reference means that one cell refers or reflects the values from another cell (usually contains a formula).
- ➔ To use a cell reference, type the cell address of the referring cell in the current cell location.
- ➔ Changing the cost of the car or interest rate, etc. will reflect a change in monthly payments.

Directions

1. Create a spreadsheet (template) with the following information.
2. Enter a formula to compute the TOTAL AVAILABLE cash in D11.
3. Use a cell reference to enter the TOTAL AVAILABLE in the DOWN PAYMENT cell (B6). Type =D11 or +D11 in cell B6.
4. Enter a formula in PRINCIPAL BORROWED to show the amount of money they need to borrow.
5. Enter a formula in MONTHLY PAYMENTS (PMT function) to show their payments every month.
6. SAVE AS: AUTO.
7. Print.
8. Change the cost of the car to $18,000 and print–not shown.
9. Change the REBATE to $500 and the TERMS IN MONTHS to 48 and print.
10. Change the INTEREST RATE to 7% and the SAVINGS to $5,800 and print.
11. Do not resave but carefully examine each printout to see the automatic adjustment in MONTHLY PAYMENTS when values are changed.

	A	B	C	D	E
1					
2	OUR NEW CAR			DOWN PAYMENT	
3					
4					
5	COST OF CAR	$21,740.00		$1,200	CASH
6	DOWN PAYMENT			$4,800	SAVINGS
7	PRINCIPAL BORROWED			$2,283	INSURANCE CHECK
8	TERMS IN MONTHS	60		$2,187	REBATE
9	INTEREST RATE	7.5%			
10	--------------------	-----------		--------	-------------------
11	MONTHLY PAYMENTS				TOTAL AVAILABLE
12					
13					
14					
15	AUTO				
16	EXERCISE 84				

Notes:

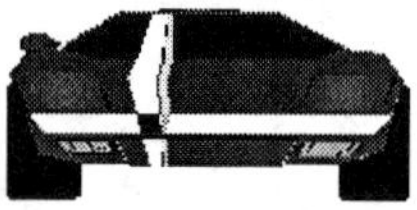

Exercise 85 - Copying a Template to a New File, Changing Values as Variables

SAVE AS: AUTO2

Michael and Vanessa have decided to look at cars from other dealers. They may decide to buy a different type of car or a used car.

Directions

1. Retrieve AUTO.
2. Copy the template of AUTO (the entire spreadsheet) to a new file. Close the file AUTO.
3. Check all formulas to make sure they have adjusted properly.
4. They have also considered buying a *used* car. Change the price of the car to $8,000. Watch the payments automatically adjust.
5. Change the TERMS IN MONTHS to 48; change the INTEREST RATE to 9%; change the savings to $2,000 and enter rebate, cash and insurance at 0. Check the monthly payments.
6. SAVE AS: AUTO 2.
7. Print the model.

	A	B	C	D	E
1					
2	OUR NEW CAR			DOWN PAYMENT	
3					
4					
5	COST OF CAR	$8,000.00		$0	CASH
6	DOWN PAYMENT			$2,000	SAVINGS
7	PRINCIPAL BORROWED			$0	INSURANCE CHECK
8	TERMS IN MONTHS	48		$0	REBATE
9	INTEREST RATE	9.0%			
10	--------------------	-----------		--------	-------------------
11	MONTHLY PAYMENTS				TOTAL AVAILABLE
12					
13					
14					
15	AUTO				
16	EXERCISE 85				

8. Now change the price of the car again to $30,000; change the rebate to $1500; change TERMS IN MONTHS to 60; change the savings to $4,900 and the INTEREST RATE to 7%.
9. Do not resave but carefully examine each printout to see the automatic adjustment in MONTHLY PAYMENTS when values are changed.
10. Print the model.

	A	B	C	D	E
1					
2	OUR NEW CAR			DOWN PAYMENT	
3					
4					
5	COST OF CAR	$30,000.00		$0	CASH
6	DOWN PAYMENT			$4,900	SAVINGS
7	PRINCIPAL BORROWED			$0	INSURANCE CHECK
8	TERMS IN MONTHS	60		$1,500	REBATE
9	INTEREST RATE	7.0%			
10	--------------------	-----------		--------	-------------------
11	MONTHLY PAYMENTS				TOTAL AVAILABLE
12					
13					
14					
15	AUTO				
16	EXERCISE 85				

Notes:

Exercise 86 - "If" Statements, "Date" Functions, Landscape, Compressed Print

SAVE AS: ANTIQUE

Loretta Canton has decided to keep an inventory of her sales from her antique shop. She would like to keep a record of how many days she owned each item and the increase or decrease of the value from the date bought to the date sold. She also wants to compute the percent of that increase or decrease and the discount on each item.

HELPFUL HINTS

➔ Range commands affect only the range you are working on.
➔ You may get negatives in this spreadsheet.

Directions

1. Create the spreadsheet as shown.
2. Center align all labels as a global command.
3. Enter a formula in F8 to compute DAYS OWNED (Date Bought from Date Sold) and copy down column F.
4. Enter a formula in G8 to compute the INCREASE or DECREASE in value from bought price to sold price and copy down column G.
5. Enter a formula in H8 to compute the PERCENT of the INCREASE or DECREASE and copy down column H.
6. Enter an "If" statement in I8 to show the discount of the antique. If the percent of the increase was 30% or higher, subtract $20 from the Sold Price. If the increase is not higher than 30% subtract $5 from the Sold Price and copy down the formula.
7. Enter a formula in C23 to compute TOTALS and copy to E23..H23.
8. Enter a formula in C24 to compute AVERAGES and copy to E24..H24.
9. Format columns C, E, and G for currency with no decimal places.
10. Format column H for percent with no decimal places.
11. Change fonts, bold, etc. at your discretion.
12. SAVE AS: ANTIQUE.
13. Print in landscape with compressed print.

	A	B	C	D	E	F	G	H	I
1			LORETTA'S ANTIQUE SHOP						
2			NEW YORK, NEW YORK						
3			INVENTORY SOLD						
4									
5		DATE	PURCHASE	DATE	SOLD	DAYS	$ INCREASE	PERCENT OF	
6	ITEM	BOUGHT	PRICE	SOLD	PRICE	OWNED	OR DECREASE	INC. OR DEC.	DISCOUNT
7									
8	TIFFANY LAMP	15-Mar-62	$375	7-Feb-90	$765				
9	ROSEWOOD TABLES	5-Jun-27	$1,035	10-Sep-91	$2,400				
10	BOTTLES	10-Sep-50	$129	1-Nov-88	$66				
11	VASE	1-Jan-63	$1,169	23-Dec-95	$450				
12	RADIO	22-Nov-45	$387	27-Jan-86	$565				
13	DESK	2-Apr-89	$1,024	14-Aug-94	$1,900				
14	TELEPHONE	12-May-55	$125	24-May-91	$285				
15	BRACELET	17-May-35	$3,055	20-Dec-87	$7,500				
16	WATCH	3-Sep-77	$190	25-Mar-90	$85				
17	CLOCK	23-Dec-84	$2,999	20-Jun-92	$3,099				
18	WASHINGTON CHAIR	3-Nov-39	$485	16-Apr-95	$775				
19	DOLLS	20-Jan-48	$500	12-Apr-92	$2,350				
20	PICTURE FRAMES	7-Mar-73	$200	11-Mar-91	$250				
21	TOY TRAINS	11-Aug-57	$450	18-Jun-94	$975				
22									
23	TOTAL								
24	AVERAGE								
25									
26									
27	ANTIQUES								
28	EXERCISE 86								

Notes:

$ Exercise 87 - Concepts Summary Exercise

SAVE AS: EQUITY

The home that Michael and Vanessa purchased is 22 years old and needs some minor repairs; therefore, they have decided to take an equity loan to make several improvements to their home. They also would like to add a wooden deck and an above ground pool. They would like to create a template to compute monthly payments.

They have decided that they can not afford more than $500 a month for more than 60 months but would like to know the monthly payments for 48 months first.

Directions

1. Create a spreadsheet that would be a template including the following information:

Amount Borrowed	$24,000
Interest Rate	11.5%
Terms in Months	48
Monthly Payments	

2. After you have created the template, enter a formula to compute monthly payments.
3. Print.
4. They thought they could borrow $24,000 but after doing the template, they realized that the payments were higher than $500.
5. Change the interest rate to 11%.
6. Change the amount borrowed until their payments are $500 or under.
7. Approximately how much can Vanessa and Michael borrow for their home improvements?
8. SAVE AS: EQUITY.
9. Print.

Notes:

$ Exercise 88 - Concepts Summary Exercise

SAVE AS: BONUS

The Josenberg Appliance Company had an excellent month in sales. In most departments, their actual sales were much higher than their projected sales for the month of April. Mrs. Josenberg would like to give her employees a bonus for all their hard work. An "If" statement would be very useful in determining bonuses for these employees.

Directions

1. Create a spreadsheet with the following information.

NAME	DEPARTMENT	PROJECTED SALES	ACTUAL SALES
SAMUELS, FRED	WASHERS	48000	63000
MCCREA, TOM	DRYERS	50000	48000
RILEY, ERIC	TELEVISIONS	50000	71000
BRADSHAW, DEBBIE	VCRs	47000	57000
BERUE, DARREN	AUDIO	50000	61000
WATERS, KRISTIN	VIDEO	45000	72000
CHU, CORASON	REFRIGERATORS	50000	46000
MCALISTER, SHARYN	STOVES	48000	53000
CZEWSKI, BILL	DISHWASHERS	50000	62000
WRIGHT, EARL	MICROWAVES	47000	37000
DAWSON, STACEY	COMPUTERS	50000	67000
MOSE, ADAM	SPEAKERS	42000	58000
HIGGINS, LUANN	COMPACTORS	48000	41000

2. Enter a formula for the following:

   - The INCREASE or DECREASE (the difference) between the projected and actual sales.
   - The PERCENT of the INCREASE or DECREASE.
   - Create an “If” statement to compute BONUS to show if the salespersons had an increase from Actual Sales to Projected Sales of 20% or higher, they received a bonus of 5% of the ACTUAL SALE. If they sold less than a 20% increase, they received no bonus or 0 (zero) in the cell.

3. Also enter formulas for the following:

   - TOTALS for PROJECTED SALES, ACTUAL SALES, INCREASE or DECREASE, PERCENT of the INCREASE or DECREASE.
   - AVERAGES for PROJECTED SALES, ACTUAL SALES, INCREASE or DECREASE, PERCENT of the INCREASE or DECREASE and BONUS.

4. Add appearance changes at your discretion.
5. SAVE AS: BONUS.
6. Print in landscape with gridlines.

Competencies:

After completing this unit, you will know how to:

1. Enter “If” statements
2. Enter “Date” functions
3. Create advanced formulas and functions
4. Insert and delete rows and columns
5. Create and copy a template
6. Enter global settings
7. Create “PMT” functions
8. Split the screen
9. Use windows

UNIT 11

Concepts:

Creating a database
Entering fields and records
Sorting in Ascending and Descending Order
Query
Changing, Adding and Deleting records
Input, Output, and Criteria Range

Points to Remember:

- A database is a collection of related information that is organized and stored in rows and columns. Some examples of databases are as follows: a telephone book, an address book, a recipe file, patient lists, etc.
- Databases contain fields and records. Column headings are field names.
- Fields are pieces of information (the smallest unit); for example, last name, first name, address, city, state, zip, phone, birthday, etc.
- Records contain the data entered into the fields; for example, Smith, John, 23 Maple Street, Springfield, PA, 876-9890, 2/17/58.
- Each row represents one record and each column represents a field.
- When typing a database leave a blank row above and below the records but do not enter any blank rows between the records.
- Records generally represent one person or object and contain information about that person or object.
- Most electronic spreadsheet software programs allow the user to create, sort, and query (search) the database.
- Records can also be sorted in ascending (A-Z) or descending (Z-A) order based on one or two specified fields. A two-level sort (secondary key) permits the user to create a sort within a sort; for example, the user can sort first names within last names.

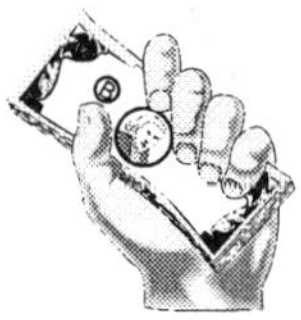

Exercise 89 - Sorting in Ascending and Descending Order

RESAVE AS: SALARY

The company would like to keep a record of those employees who are making the highest Gross Pay. They also would like a record of the lowest to the highest hourly rate and the employees' names sorted in ascending order.

HELPFUL HINTS

➔ Remember when highlighting the records to include all the parts of all the records in the database.
➔ Formulas will adjust when sorting.
➔ Once a database has been sorted, it cannot be unsorted except with undo.
➔ Databases should have a blank row above and below the database.

Directions

1. Retrieve SALARY.
2. Insert a blank row 17.
3. Sort on NAME in ascending order – not shown.
4. Print.
5. Sort on HOURLY RATE in ascending order from the lowest to the highest hourly rate – not shown.
6. Print.
7. Sort on GROSS PAY in descending order from the highest to the lowest GROSS PAY.
8. Print.
9. SAVE AS: SALARY.
10. Make formatting changes to your discretion.
11. The illustration shows last sort only.

	A	B	C	D	E	F
1	SALARY REPORT					
2	WEEK ENDING MAY 30, 1996					
3						
4	SOCIAL SECURITY		DATE	TOTAL	HOURLY	GROSS
5	NUMBER	NAME	HIRED	HOURS	RATE	PAY
6						
7	342-76-9981	*ROYCHOUD, ALBERT*	5/17/69	47	$22.67	$1,065.49
8	997-89-2343	*POLINOWSKI, SUSAN*	11/12/92	40	$14.75	$590.00
9	769-31-5432	*WHEAT, CINDERELLA*	4/29/80	40	$13.95	$558.00
10	547-76-3211	*SCHER, EVELYN*	4/9/94	30	$15.25	$457.50
11	665-65-7654	*HIBBERD, BETSY*	6/5/88	35	$12.65	$442.75
12	123-78-9087	*THOMPSON, JAMES*	1/14/82	40	$9.25	$370.00
13	357-63-0070	*ALYANAKIAN, LOUIS*	12/19/83	32	$11.55	$369.60
14	231-98-6665	*THOMPSON, CHRIS*	5/23/95	44	$7.75	$341.00
15	665-01-0041	*GREY, EVELYN*	5/25/95	36	$8.10	$291.60
16	411-12-0700	*GRAILNIK, SHIRLEY*	2/22/94	27	$10.35	$279.45
17						
18	TOTAL			371	$126.27	$4,765.39
19	AVERAGE			37	$12.63	$476.54
20	LOWEST			27	$7.75	$279.45
21	HIGHEST			47	$22.67	$1,065.49
22						
23	SALARY					
24	EXERCISE 89					

Notes:

Exercise 90 - Creating a Database, Sorting in Ascending and Descending Order

RESAVE AS: CARS

The owner of Bill's A-1 Used Cars would like more organized records. He would like his database sorted by the salespersons' names and he would also like to know who had the highest sales *each* month.

HELPFUL HINTS

- ➔ When entering the database, always put the field names as the column headings.
- ➔ There should be no blank rows between records.
- ➔ Some software programs select the first field to sort as the primary key and the second field to sort as the secondary key.

Directions

1. Retrieve CARS.
2. Sort the field SALESREP in ascending order. This will alphabetize the salespersons so they can be located easier - not shown.
3. Print.
4. Sort the JANUARY field in descending order to see the highest to the lowest sales for that month–not shown.
5. Print the database.
6. Sort to show *highest to lowest* for FEBRUARY – not shown.
7. Print.
8. Also sort to show *highest to the lowest* for the month of MARCH.
9. Print.
10. RESAVE AS: CARS.
11. The illustration below only shows the last sort.

	A	B	C	D	E
1	BILL'S A-1 USED CARS				
2	SALESPEOPLE REPORT				
3	FIRST QUARTER				
4	TOTAL CARS SOLD				
5					
6	SALESREP	JANUARY	FEBRUARY	MARCH	TOTALS
7					
8	KLOPP	17	22	27	
9	SULLIVAN	21	24	23	
10	LOMBARDO	22	19	20	
11	PARKER	15	17	19	
12	GUNKLE	18	19	18	
13	WESTON	19	18	17	
14	ASSOUSA	15	16	16	
15	COCHRAN	5	9	15	
16	ULLMAN	13	14	12	
17	BELL	11	12	10	
18	PILIO	12	15	9	
19	SHADE	15	15	5	
20					
21	TOTAL				
22	AVERAGE				
23	MINUMUM				
24	MAXIMUM				
25					
26	CARS				
27	EXERCISE 90				

Notes:

Exercise 91 - Creating a Database, Sorting in Ascending and Descending Order, Updating Records

SAVE AS: JFK

The registrar at John F. Kennedy University has recently decided to computerize the student database. He will begin by entering a few students and later he will delete, update (change), or add new information. This database will be available to all staff members at the university.

Directions

1. Enter the spreadsheet as shown.

	A	B	C	D
1	JOHN F. KENNEDY UNIVERSITY			
2	STUDENT PLACEMENT			
3				
4	NAME	S.S.NO.	CITY, STATE	MAJOR
5				
6	SWANTKO, PENELOPE	886-23-0605	CHICAGO, ILLINOIS	HISTORY
7	MASON, PAM	878-76-1111	SPRINGFIELD, MASSACHUSETTS	CHEMISTRY
8	BELLY, CECIL	787-09-7634	BOISE, IDAHO	CHEMISTRY
9	BARRETT, BEN	767-77-0155	NASHVILLE, TENNESSEE	HISTORY
10	COLAIEZZI, ROBERT	654-88-7612	NOME, ALASKA	BIOLOGY
11	REDAMER, DAVID	654-43-9000	DOVER, DELAWARE	ENGLISH
12	SWANTKO, FRANCIS	555-43-8712	AUSTIN, TEXAS	ACCOUNTING
13	ADLER, RACHEAL	438-74-2368	RAYSTOWN, PENNSYLVANIA	BIOLOGY
14	GROGAN, KAREN	842-987-0087	NOME, ALASKA	ANTHROPOLOGY
15	JABLOWSKI, SUSAN	232-90-7766	WYNWOOD, CALIFORNIA	CHEMISTRY
16	NEIGH, DAWN	231-87-5430	OMAHA, NEBRASKA	ACCOUNTING
17	MCALLISTER, STACY	180-99-8765	NASHVILLE, TENNESSEE	BIOLOGY
18	IWASAKI, SETH	156-44-0112	BELMONT, NEW JERSEY	ENGINEERING
19	JABLOWSKI, FRED	121-89-2213	SPRINGFIELD, MASSACHUSETTS	PHILOSOPHY
20				
21	JFK			
22	EXERCISE 91			

2. Sort in ascending order by the field NAME.
3. Print.
4. Karen Grogan has quit the University. Delete her record.
5. Add three new students: Plum, Krista Lynn, 121-98-9876, Pittsburgh, Pennsylvania, Anthropology; Battaglia, Mary, 191-98-7654, Nome, Alaska, Chemistry; McAllister, Melissa, 871-11-1231, Nome, Alaska, Engineering.
6. Dawn Neigh has recently married and her new last name is Groves.
7. Sort in descending order by major.
8. Print.
9. Sort the field NAME in ascending order again after all changes have been made.
10. SAVE AS: JFK.
11. Print with gridlines.

Exercise 92 - Sorting, Two Level Sort (Primary and Secondary) Criteria Range, Input and Output Range

SAVE AS: JFK2

The registrar will need to alphabetize the students by major and by name.

HELPFUL HINTS

➔ The input range is the range you are searching; the criteria range is the specific information you are searching for and the output range is the range where the extracted criteria will go.
➔ Two level sorts are sorts within a sort.
➔ When sorting a database, make sure all of the parts of each record *stay together*.

Directions

1. Retrieve JFK.
2. Sort by City, State in descending order – not shown.
3. Print.
4. Sort by Name in ascending order as the first sort and Major in ascending order as second sort–not shown.
5. Print.
6. Sort by Major in descending order as first sort and Name in ascending order as second sort – not shown.
7. Print.
8. Delete Melissa McAllister's record. She has left the university.
9. Krista Plum and Cecil Belly have both changed their Major to Biology. Change their records.
10. Sort again as a first sort on City, State in ascending order and second sort on Major in ascending order – illustrated below.
11. SAVE AS: JFK2.

12. Set an input range as the entire spreadsheet and the criteria to search for all the students from Nome, Alaska. Set an output range as a separate range – include all fields.
13. Print only the output range – not shown.
14. SAVE AS: JFK2.

	A	B	C	D
1	HN F. KENNEDY UNIVERSITY			
2	STUDENT PLACEMENT			
3				
4	NAME	S.S.NO.	CITY, STATE	MAJOR
5				
6	SWANTKO, FRANCIS	555-43-8712	AUSTIN, TEXAS	ACCOUNTING
7	IWASAKI, SETH	156-44-0112	BELMONT, NEW JERSEY	ENGINEERING
8	BELLY, CECIL	787-09-7634	BOISE, IDAHO	CHEMISTRY
9	SWANTKO, PENELOPE	886-23-0605	CHICAGO, ILLINOIS	HISTORY
10	REDAMER, DAVID	654-43-9000	DOVER, DELAWARE	ENGLISH
11	MCALLISTER, STACY	180-99-8765	NASHVILLE, TENNESSEE	BIOLOGY
12	BARRETT, BEN	767-77-0155	NASHVILLE, TENNESSEE	HISTORY
13	COLAIEZZI, ROBERT	654-88-7612	NOME, ALASKA	BIOLOGY
14	BATTAGLIA, MARY	191-98-7654	NOME, ALASKA	CHEMISTRY
15	GROVES, DAWN	231-87-5430	OMAHA, NEBRASKA	ACCOUNTING
16	PLUM, KRISTA	121-98-9876	PITTSBURGH, PENNSYLVANIA	BIOLOGY
17	ADLER, RACHEAL	438-74-2368	RAYSTOWN, PENNSYLVANIA	BIOLOGY
18	MASON, PAM	878-76-1111	SPRINGFIELD, MASSACHUSETTS	CHEMISTRY
19	JABLOWSKI, FRED	121-89-2213	SPRINGFIELD, MASSACHUSETTS	PHILOSOPHY
20	JABLOWSKI, SUSAN	232-90-7766	WYNWOOD, CALIFORNIA	CHEMISTRY
21				
22				
23				
24				
25				
26	JFK			
27	EXERCISE 92			

Notes:

Exercise 93 - Sorting, Two Level Sort, Input, Output, and Criteria Range

RESAVE AS: DOLLS

Cupie's doll collection would be more organized if it were sorted to locate the dolls more quickly. She would also like to be able to find specific information about each; for example, a printed list of each doll that is porcelain, etc.

Directions

1. Retrieve DOLLS.
2. Sort by DATE BOUGHT in descending order – not shown.
3. Print.
4. Sort by DOLL in ascending order as the first sort and by PRESENT VALUE as the second sort – not shown.
5. Print.
6. Sort by BRAND in ascending order as the first sort and by VALUE AT PURCHASE in ascending order as the second sort–illustrated below.
7. Print.
8. RESAVE AS: DOLLS
9. Set an input range as the entire spreadsheet and set the criteria range to search for all the dolls with the special feature of HUMAN HAIR. Set an output range as a separate range. Include all fields in the output range. Print the output range only.
10. Set an input range as the entire spreadsheet and the criteria will be to search for all the dolls that are porcelain *and* are DIMPLES, INC. Set an output range as a separate range. Include all fields in the output range. Print *only* the output range.
11. Set an input range as the entire spreadsheet and the criteria will be to search for all the dolls that are made by MADAM SANDRA and cost more than $50. Set an output range as a separate range. Include all fields in the output range. Print *only* the output range.
12. Do not resave.

	A	B	C	D	E	F	G	H	I
1	CUPIE GERBER'S DOLL COLLECTION								
2									
3			SPECIAL	DATE	VALUE AT	PRESENT	INC./DEC.	PERCENT	
4	BRAND	DOLL	FEATURES	BOUGHT	PURCHASE	VALUE	VALUE	INC./DEC.	TAX
5									
6	BETTY'S BABIES	JUDY GARLAND	OPEN MOUTH	Jun-63	$40	$155			
7	BETTY'S BABIES	SHIRLEY TEMPLE	HUMAN HAIR	Jan-65	$62	$165			
8	BETTY'S BABIES	NEWBORN TWINS	BENDABLE	Nov-83	$65	$47			
9	BETTY'S BABIES	SPANKY	OPEN MOUTH	Apr-80	$78	$145			
10	DIMPLES, INC.	JOHN F. KENNEDY	PORCELAIN	Sep-70	$23	$125			
11	DIMPLES, INC.	MARILYN MONROE	PORCELAIN	May-70	$32	$113			
12	DIMPLES, INC.	CARY GRANT	SILK SUIT	Jun-63	$41	$111			
13	DIMPLES, INC.	SANDRA LEE	LACE	May-70	$82	$44			
14	MADAM SANDRA	ROMEO	SILK SHIRT	Mar-69	$25	$87			
15	MADAM SANDRA	JULIETTE	ALL LACE	Feb-81	$32	$96			
16	MADAM SANDRA	JOSEPHINE	HUMAN HAIR	May-90	$42	$47			
17	MADAM SANDRA	CLEOPATRA	DIAMONDS	Jul-92	$45	$72			
18	MADAM SANDRA	NAPOLEON	BENDABLE	May-90	$55	$61			
19	MADAM SANDRA	QUEEN ELIZABETH	DIAMONDS	Aug-94	$50	$90			
20									
21	TOTAL								
22									
23	DOLL								
24	EXERCISE 93								

Notes:

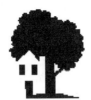

Exercise 94 - Concepts Summary Exercise

SAVE AS: HOMES

The American Dream Real Estate Company has developed a computerized database of its homes that are on the market. The company receives many inquiries about these homes everyday. To speed the response to these inquiries (queries), this database at times needs sorting and updating.

Directions

1. Enter the large database as shown directly into the computer.

					AMERICAN DREAM REAL ESTATE		
NUMBER	SALEPERSON	TYPE HOME	LOT SIZE	SPECIAL FEATURE	SPECIAL FEATURE	ROOMS	BEDROOMS
************	******************	**********************	*****************	*******************************	**********************************	**********	***************
234	TIMM	SPLIT LEVEL	1/2 ACRE	FIREPLACE--LR	FINISHED FAMILY ROOM	7	3
235	MCALLISTER	RANCH	4 ACRE	FIREPLACE--FR	SWIMMING POOL	10	4
236	RIVERO	CONTEMPORARY	2 ACRES	WOODED LOT	HIGH CEILINGS	10	4
237	RIVERO	COLONIAL	1 ACRE	2 FIREPLACES	LARGE MASTER	9	4
238	RICCI	BILEVEL	1/3 ACRE	FAMILY ROOM	WET BAR	8	3
239	LONG	STONE COLONIA	6 ACRES	FAMILY ROOM	WOODED LOT	14	5
240	CALLAGHAN	CONDOMINIUM	STRUCTURE	MAINTENANCE	SWIMMING POOL	6	2
241	HARRISON	RANCH	2 1/2 ACRES	SWIMMING POOL	LARGE WOODEN DECK	11	5
242	TIMM	COLONIAL	3 ACRES	FINISHED DECK	FIREPLACE-BR	10	4
243	GANNON	BILEVEL	1 ACRE	PANELED KITCHEN	CUL DE SAC	8	3
244	MCALLISTER	CONDOMINIUM	STRUCTURE	TENNIS COURT	MAINTENANCE	7	3
245	LONG	CONDOMINIUM	STRUCTURE	SWIMMING POOL	TENNIS COURT	7	2
246	LONG	TOWN HOUSE	1/5 ACRE	STONE STRUCTURE	CUL DE SAC	8	2
247	MCALLISTER	SPLIT LEVEL	1 ACRE	WOODEN DECK	SWIMMING POOL	9	4
248	RICCI	RANCH	2 ACRES	WOODED LOT	CUL DE SAC	12	5
249	CALLAGHAN	RANCH	1/4 ACRE	GARAGE	QUIET STREET	8	3
250	LONG	CONTEMPOARY	1 1/2 ACRE	3 FIREPLACES	LARGE FINISHED DECK	11	4
251	CALLAGHAN	TOWN HOUSE	1/6 ACRE	GARAGE	TENNIS COURTS	8	3
252	HARRISON	TOWN HOUSE	1/5 ACRE	HIGH CEILINGS	FIREPLACE--LR	7	3
253	MCALLISTER	STONE RANCH	4 ACRES	CATHEDRAL CEILINGS	WOODED LOT	12	5
254	GANNON	COLONIAL	3 ACRES	CATHEDRAL CEILINGS	3 FIREPLACES	11	4

NUMBER	BATHS	ADDRESS	TOWN	OWNERS	ASKING PRICE	WILL ACCEPT
***********	*******	******************************	********************	***	****************	****************
234	2	121 STERN STREET	BROOMALL	JUSTIN & CELESTE CAMPENELLI	$202,000	$200,000
235	3	34 WEST KENNEDY	SPRINGFIELD	DR. CHRISTOPHER STAHLEY	$500,000	$475,000
236	3	ONE SPROUL ROAD	SPRINGFIELD	CORY & JESSICA DINGELHOPPER	$350,000	$335,000
237	3	77 SLAB ROAD	WAYNE	MERCEDES WALLINGFORD	$147,000	$146,000
238	2	989 HIGHWOODS AVE.	SMITHBRIDGE	FLAVION AND KRISTA MANCINI	$104,000	$99,000
239	4	23 DEVON LANE	WAYNE	FRED LABATH	$490,000	$480,000
240	2	1145 ROCKLAND AVE.	DARBY	SAM & SUSAN SNOWFLAKE	$97,000	$94,000
241	3	457 BAILEY ST.	SMITHBRIDGE	MARCIA JOHNSON	$276,000	$275,000
242	3	TWO TERRENCE LANE	BROOKHAVEN	MR. AND MRS. WALTER SARKEES	$380,000	$367,000
243	2	988 LINCOLN AVE.	MONACA	MELISSA & STEVE STRETCH	$132,000	$130,000
244	3	555 DELVER CIRCLE	BLOOMFIELD	ELEANOR AND HARRY THOMPSON	$168,000	$157,000
245	2	450 GESNER AVE.	DREXEL	MEGAN & MIKE McCARTHY	$111,000	$109,000
246	2	807 MASON ROAD	TAYLOR TOWN	ROSEMARY LAMBERT	$90,000	$87,000
247	3	42 SABINE AVE.	CLOVER	LINDA & JOHN SHILLINGSBURG	$178,000	$175,000
248	4	ONE COBB ROAD	DARBY	ANGELA & GREG BIENKOWSKI	$320,000	$290,000
249	2	99 CHIPMUNK LANE	SPRINGFIELD	DR. BEAU BRENDLEY	$167,000	$156,000
250	3	67 WOODLAND AVE.	MONACA	DR. VICKI BABISH	$330,000	$302,000
251	2	66 KEYSTONE ROAD	RIVER HILLS	SISTER MARY MAGARET CELLINI	$120,000	$115,000
252	2	100 SUMMIT LANE	DELTA	VALERIE & RICH BOLEY	$209,000	$206,000
253	4	30 CHERRY CIRLCE	SUGAR TOWN	JOHN AND DIANE CLARKE	$550,000	$535,000
254	3	55 WINDEMERE LANE	MONACA	J. D. KAHLER	$403,000	$401,000

2. Sort by number of ROOMS in descending order as the first sort and TOWN in ascending order as the second sort.
3. Print the entire spreadsheet in landscape and compressed.
4. Sort by ASKING PRICE in ascending order as the first sort and by TOWN in descending order as the second sort.
5. Print in landscape and compressed.
6. Make the following changes: ANGELA AND GREG BIENKOWSKI (number 248) have lowered the price of their home. Change their Asking Price to $300,000 and the WILL ACCEPT price to $275,000.
7. Change the asking price on house listing number 252 to $185,000 and change WILL ACCEPT $178,000.
8. Sort by ROOMS in ascending order as first sort and ASKING PRICE in ascending order as the second sort.
9. Print.
10. SAVE AS: HOMES.

Exercise 95 - Concepts Summary Exercise

RESAVE AS: HOMES

Information from the database of HOMES needs to be extracted and printed on separate pages for several customers. After the information is extracted, it should also be sorted for easy illustration.

Directions

1. Retrieve HOMES.
2. Ethel and Fred Nertz have met with a realtor and asked for several printouts with various specifications.
3. Choose the entire spreadsheet as the input range.
4. Select an output range of your choice. Include all fields in each search.
5. They have asked (criteria range) for the following printouts:

    - All homes in Springfield.
    - All homes with a cathedral ceiling.
    - All homes with 5 bedrooms.
    - All homes with 7 or more rooms and 3 or more bathrooms.
    - All homes with a swimming pool and will accept less than $300,000.
    - All homes with a wooden deck or a tennis court.

6. Print each of the searches on separate pages.
7. Sort each search by ASKING PRICE in ascending order.
8. RESAVE AS: HOMES.

Notes:

Competencies

After completing this unit, you will know how to:

1. Create a database
2. Enter fields and records
3. Update records — change, add or delete information
4. Sort in ascending and descending order
5. Create an input, output and criteria range
6. Print the output

UNIT 12

Concepts:

Creating a Pie, Line, and Column Chart
Legends and Titles on a Chart
Embedding a Chart on a Spreadsheet
Data Labels
Changing the Y-axis Scale
Charting with one or multiple variables
Sizing the Chart

Points to Remember:

- Chart types can be column, bar, pie, stacked bar, etc.
- When creating a second chart of any type, change the type to create an entire new chart and the legends, titles, data labels, etc. will remain the same.
- The X-axis is the horizontal bottom of the chart.
- The Y-axis is the vertical edge of the chart (can also be called vertical values).
- The *scale* of the Y-axis is the increments of values.
- Legends are descriptions assigned to ranges.
- There can be a title on a chart.
- Charts can be embedded within the spreadsheet or they can be entered on another page.
- Data labels are text or values that can be added to specific points *on* a chart.

Exercise 96 - Creating a Pie Chart, Legends, Chart Title

SAVE AS: FUND

Bob has given much thought to his investment strategies. He will keep a record of each investment and will watch the changes in these investments from time to time. A pie chart will illustrate Bob's percent invested in each different account.

HELPFUL HINTS

- ➔ The X-axis is horizontal and the Y-axis is vertical.
- ➔ Some electronic software programs have wizards that make creating a chart very easy.
- ➔ Every time you change a value in your spreadsheet, the chart automatically adjusts to reflect that change.

Directions

1. Enter the spreadsheet as shown.
2. Create a pie chart to reflect the spreadsheet using the range A6..B12.
3. The range A6..A12 contains the legends (labels that describe the values) for the pie chart. Enter the legend of MANNING as A6, etc.
4. Add the title, BOB'S STOCK FUND.
5. Embed the pie chart on the spreadsheet.
6. Size the chart at your discretion.
7. Look at the percent of each investment — the pie chart is based on 100%.
8. SAVE AS: FUND.
9. Print the chart and the spreadsheet. (The chart may be visible on your screen in color. If you have a color printer, you can print the chart and the spreadsheet in color.)
10. Change financial growth to $14,000 and watch the chart adjust to the change — not shown.
11. RESAVE AS: FUND.

	A	B	C	D	E	F
1	BOB'S STOCK FUND					
2						
3	FUND	TOTAL				
4		COST				
5						
6	MANNING	$ 28,600.00				
7	HEALTH & SCIENCE	$ 17,900.00				
8	FOUNDERS	$ 22,000.00				
9	FINANCE SERVICES	$ 5,000.00				
10	FINANCIAL GROWTH	$ 19,000.00				
11	LONG TERM FUND	$ 22,000.00				
12	BRODY FUND	$ 8,600.00				
13						
14	FUND					
15	EXERCISE 96					
16						
17						
18						
19						
20						
21						
22						
23						
24						
25						
26						
27						
28						
29						
30						
31						
32						
33						
34						
35						

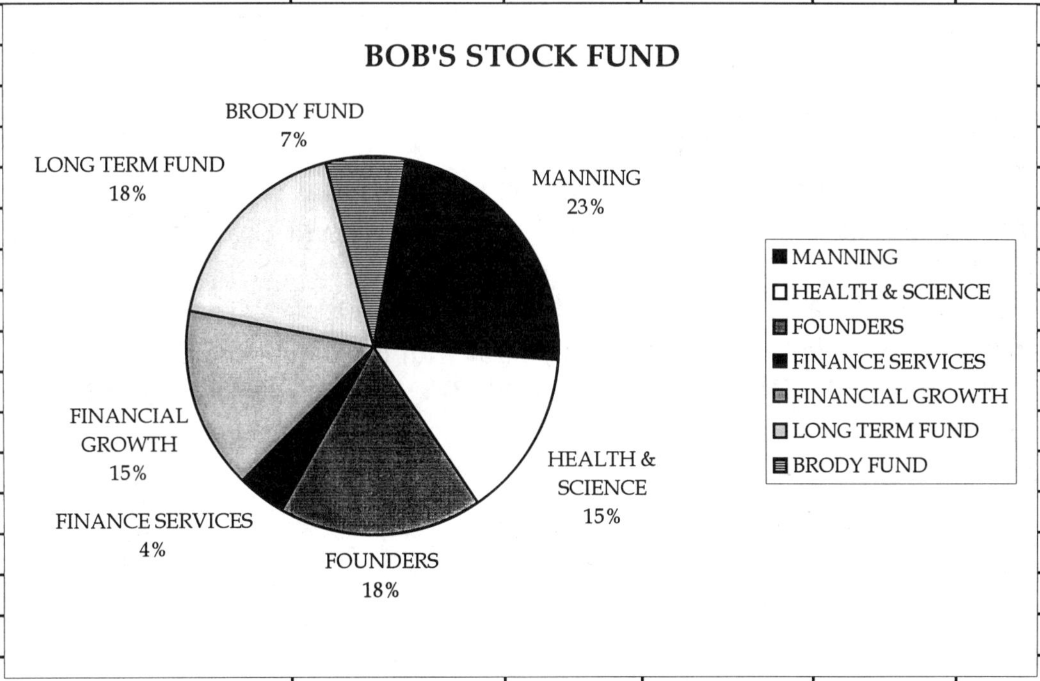

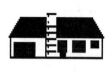

Exercise 97 - Creating a Pie and Column Chart, Legends, X-and Y-axis Titles, Chart Title

SAVE AS: FAMILY

It is a good idea for many families and individuals to be on a budget. Household expenses are endless and ever growing. For many individuals, a budget can help control spending. Create a pie chart and a column chart that show the percent of each expense for the Martin family for the year ending 1995.

This is a useful tool to help visualize the entire picture of income and expenses.

Directions

1. Enter the spreadsheet as shown.
2. Create a pie chart using the range A6..B13.
3. Enter a chart title of MARTIN BUDGET, 1995.
4. Enter legends as the items listed A6..A13–A6 as HOUSING, etc.
5. Embed the pie chart on the spreadsheet.
6. Size the chart to your discretion.
7. Print the spreadsheet and the chart.
8. Leave all the settings the same and change the pie chart type to a column chart.
9. Enter a title for the X-axis of ITEMS and the Y-axis as EXPE for expense.
10. Embed the column chart below the pie chart.
11. SAVE AS: FAMILY.
12. Print the embedded pie and column charts with the spreadsheet.
13. Change the HOUSING from $8,000 to $6,000 and watch the chart adjust to the spreadsheet.
14. Do not resave.

	A	B	C	D	E	F	G
1	THE MARTIN FAMILY'S PERSONAL BUDGET						
2	YEAR ENDING 1995						
3							
4	ITEM	EXPENSE					
5							
6	HOUSING	$ 8,000					
7	UTILITIES	$ 1,800					
8	CAR PAYMENTS	$ 2,500					
9	VACATION/ENTERTAINMENT	$ 2,200					
10	TAXES	$ 3,700					
11	CLOTHING	$ 2,500					
12	SAVINGS	$ 1,900					
13	MISCELLANEOUS	$ 3,900					
14							
15	*FAMILY*						
16	*EXERCISE 97*						

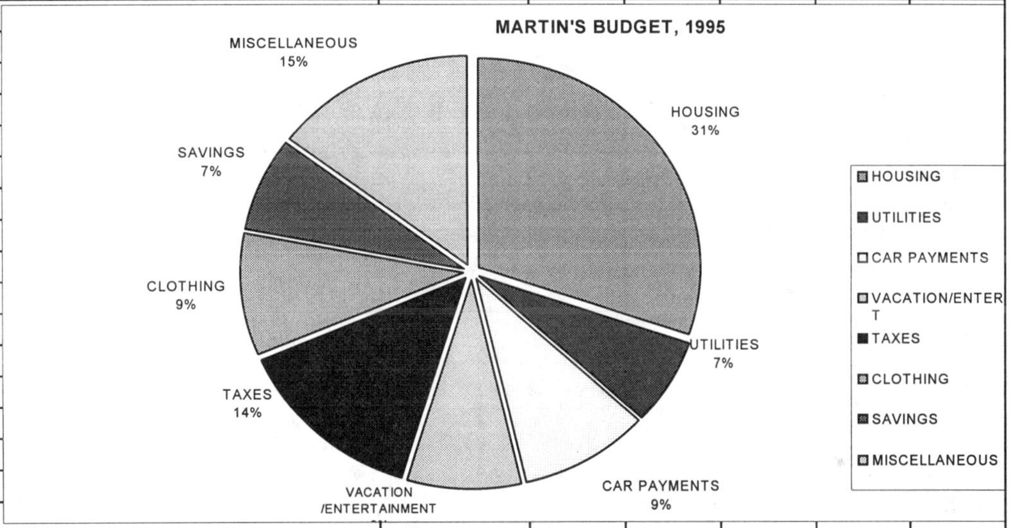

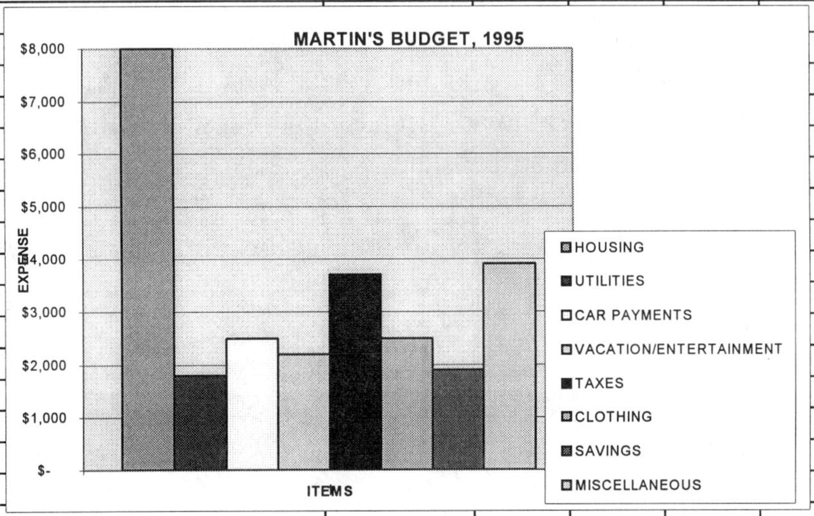

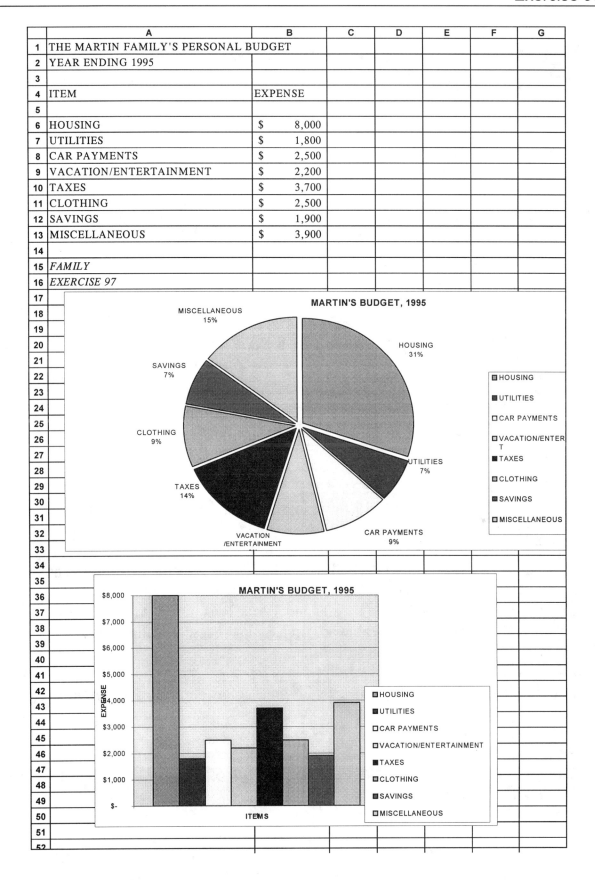

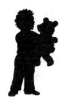

Exercise 98 - Copying a Range to a File, Column Chart, Legends, Titles, Data Labels

SAVE AS: DOLLS2

Cupie would find a chart quite useful to visualize the increase or decrease in value of each doll in her collection.

Directions

1. Retrieve DOLLS.
2. Delete column A, C, and D (BRAND, SPECIAL FEATURES, and DATE BOUGHT).
3. Also delete row 21 with TOTALS and the contents of cell A1.
4. Copy columns A, B, and C to a new file.
5. Adjust column widths.
6. SAVE AS: DOLLS2.
7. Close the original DOLLS and *do not* resave.
8. Enter the heading CUPIE'S DOLL COLLECTION in cell A1.
9. Reformat decimal places in columns B and C to show no decimal places.
10. Create a column chart using columns A, B, and C.
11. Enter a title of CUPIE'S DOLL COLLECTION on the chart.
12. The legends are SERIES 1 (VALUE AT PURCHASE—enter in a cell as shown) and SERIES 2 (PRESENT VALUE—enter in a cell).
13. Enter DOLL TYPE as the X-axis title and VALUE as the Y-axis.
14. Add data labels as values to Value at Purchase and Present Value.
15. Do not embed the chart on the spreadsheet.
16. Enter this chart on a separate page.
17. Enhance the appearance of the chart with font, color, and other appearance changes of your choice.
18. SAVE AS: DOLLS2.
19. Print only the chart.
20. Change the present value of Napoleon from $61 to $112 and watch the chart adjust to the new value. Do not resave.

CUPIE'S DOLL COLLECTION		
	VALUE AT	PRESENT
DOLL	PURCHASE	VALUE
JUDY GARLAND	$40	$155
SHIRLEY TEMPLE	$62	$165
NEWBORN TWINS	$65	$47
SPANKY	$78	$145
JOHN F. KENNEDY	$23	$125
MARILYN MONROE	$32	$113
CARY GRANT	$41	$111
SANDRA LEE	$82	$44
ROMEO	$25	$87
JULIETTE	$32	$96
JOSEPHINE	$42	$47
CLEOPATRA	$45	$72
NAPOLEON	$55	$61
QUEEN ELIZABETH	$50	$90

Notes:

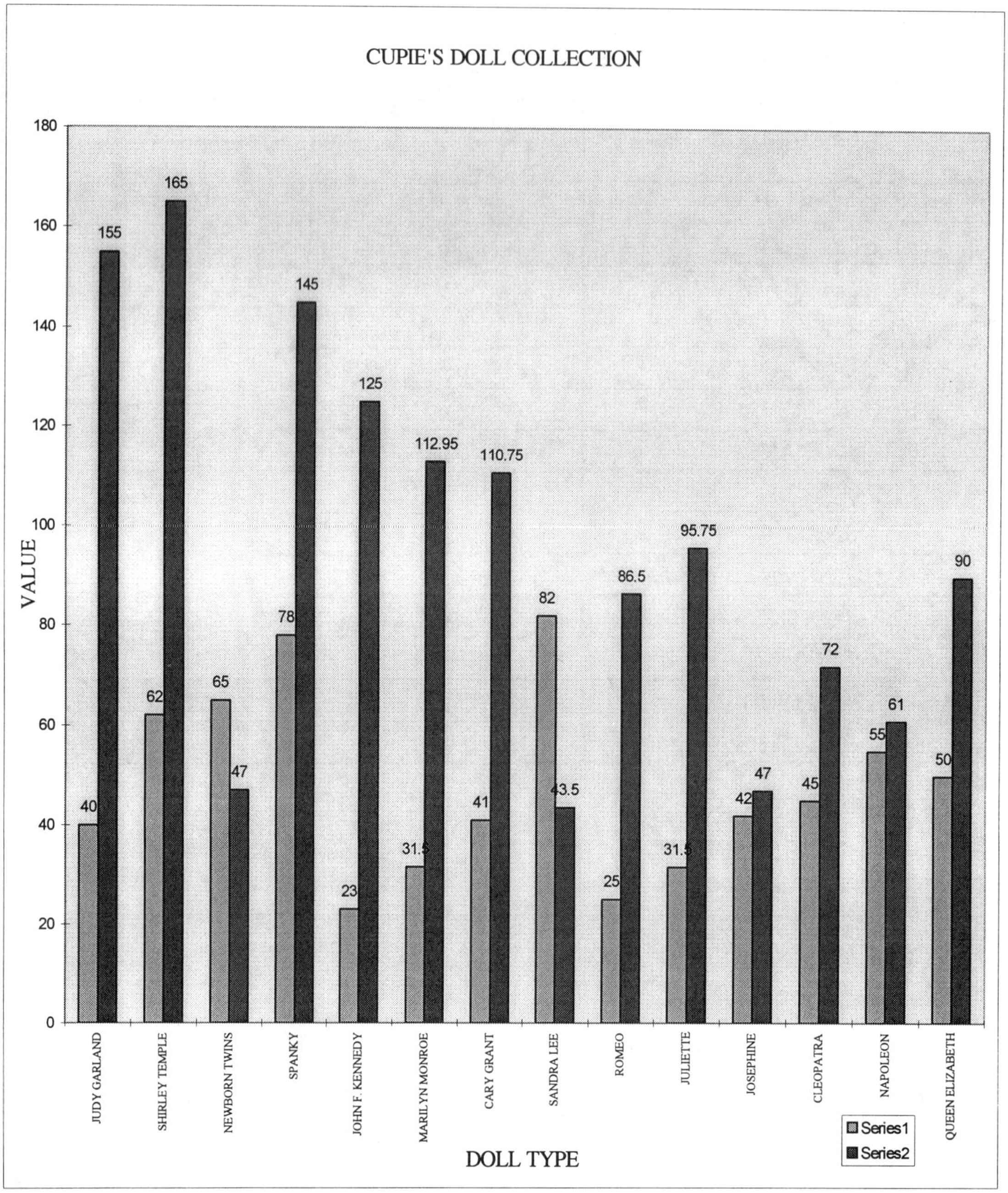

DOLLS 2
EXERCISE 98

Exercise 99 - Line Chart with Four Variables, Legends, Chart Title, X- and Y-axis Titles, Setting the Y-axis Scale

SAVE AS: FUND2

Bob has decided to track the increase or decrease of four of his funds over the first half of 1996. He will plot the change in monthly share prices.

Directions

1. Enter the spreadsheet as shown.
2. Change the point size in the first two rows.
3. Use "Date" functions from B4 to G4.
4. Create a line chart using the range A4..G8 with the fund names as legends.
5. Set the months as the X-axis and the fund price as the Y-axis.
6. Enter a chart title of SHARE PRICES PER MONTH–JANUARY TO JUNE 1996.
7. Set the Y-axis scale for 20 increments (step value of 20).
8. Enter the X-axis title as MONTHS and the Y-axis value as PRI for PRICE.
9. Embed the chart on the spreadsheet.
10. SAVE AS: FUND2.
11. Print the embedded chart and spreadsheet as illustrated.
12. Enhance the appearance of the chart with font, color, and other appearance changes of your choice.
13. Change values for MANNING for MAY-1996 to $125.50 and watch your chart automatically adjust to that change – not shown.
14. Print again.

	A	B	C	D	E	F	G
1	*BOB'S STOCK FUND--INCREASE OR DECREASE PER MONTH*						
2	*PRICES PER SHARE*						
3							
4	MONTH ENDING	Jan-96	Feb-96	Mar-96	Apr-96	May-96	Jun-96
5	MANNING	$26.75	$36.88	$44.67	$52.22	$95.60	$63.20
6	HEALTH & SCIENCE	$11.85	$9.25	$12.50	$11.55	$12.90	$14.99
7	FOUNDERS	$92.75	$121.33	$100.33	$122.67	$144.45	$135.55
8	BRODY FUND	$32.50	$29.77	$27.30	$14.90	$12.44	$13.76
9							
10	FUND2						
11	EXERCISE 99						
12							
13							
14							
15							
16							
17							
18							
19							
20							
21							
22							
23							
24							
25							
26							
27							
28							
29							
30							

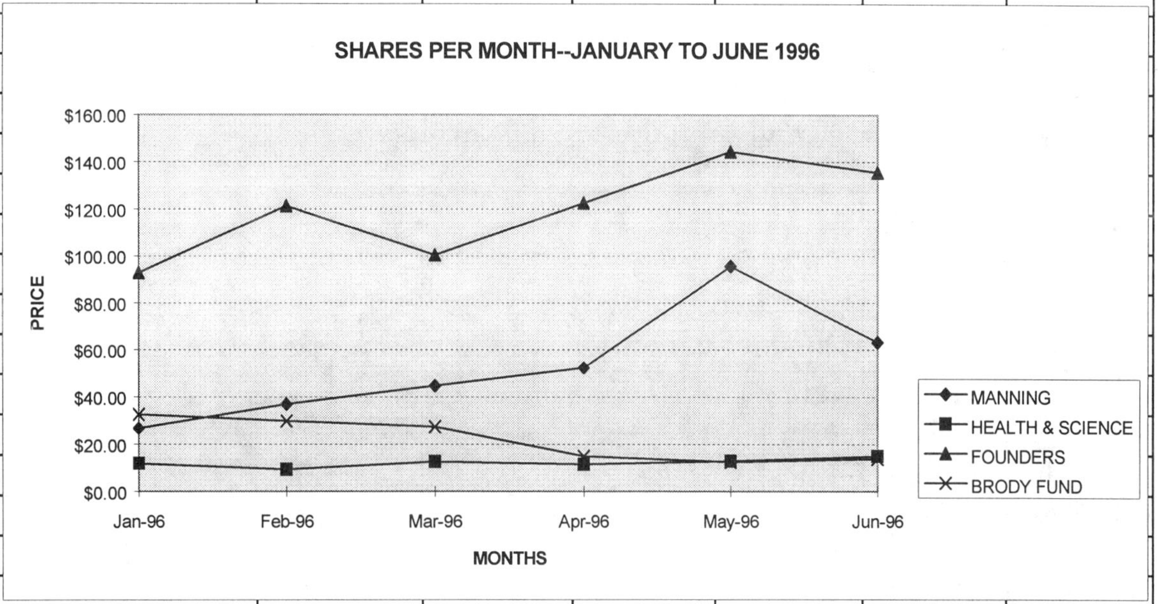

Notes:

Exercise 100 - Concepts Summary Exercise

SAVE AS: HARDWARE

Rich would like to keep track of the percent of Total Sales in each of his five departments of his hardware store. For the month of January his Total Sales for all departments was $28,000. Of that $28,000, 20% of his sales was in the Hand Tools department, 10% of that $28,000 was in the Electric Tools department, etc. The total percent column is a check for the five departments and should be 100%.

Directions

1. Create a spreadsheet with the following information.

RICH'S HARDWARE STORE							
SALES--FIRST AND SECOND QUARTER, 1996							
FIVE DEPARTMENTS							
	HAND TOOLS	ELECTRIC TOOLS	PLUMBING SUPPLIES	ELECTRICAL SUPPLIES	HOUSEWARE MATERIALS	ACTUAL TOTAL SALES	TOTAL PERCENT
JANUARY	20%	10%	19%	21%	30%	$28,000	100%
FEBRUARY	30%	15%	8%	19%	28%	$33,000	100%
MARCH	14%	16%	19%	24%	27%	$26,500	100%
APRIL	19%	20%	17%	24%	20%	$32,000	100%
MAY	23%	22%	12%	24%	19%	$34,500	100%
JUNE	22%	24%	16%	20%	18%	$37,000	100%

2. The TOTAL PERCENT column should be a function which adds all the departments' percents and should always total 100%. This is the only formula on this spreadsheet.
3. Create a column chart with the months as the X-axis and the percents as the Y-axis.
4. Add legends to identify each department (Hand Tools, Electric Tools, etc.).
5. Embed the chart on the spreadsheet. Using the chart, which department had steady increase in sales over the six months?

6. Using the chart, which department had a steady decrease in sales over the six months?
7. Which month had the highest TOTAL SALES?
8. Which department had the lowest sales in February?
9. Print the chart and the spreadsheet.
10. SAVE AS: HARDWARE.
11. Create a line chart using the same criteria as the X-axis and Y-axis, chart title, legends, etc. as was used in HARDWARE.
12. Enhance the appearance of the chart with fonts, color, and other appearance changes of your choice.
13. Enter data labels as values within the department.
14. Print only the chart.
15. RESAVE AS: HARDWAR2.

Exercise 101 - Concepts Summary Exercise

SAVE AS: ELECTRIC

Residents and businesses receive an electric and/or gas bill on a monthly basis from their local utility company. The utility company usually includes a chart which shows the *actual and estimated* usage for gas and electric for the previous year by month. This spreadsheet will create a simulated electric and gas bill with the chart included. Electric is measured in kilowatt hours (kWhs) and gas is measured in hundreds of cubic feet (Ccf).

Directions

1. Enter the information below into a spreadsheet.

RECO ENERGY			
ACCOUNT NUMBER: 23-98-76-9898			
Rate R: Electric Residence Service			
Gas Residence Service			
Meter Number 9876549898			
Customer: V. T. Babish			
from: September 27, 1996			
to: October 26, 1996			
Electric Usage	Price	Kilowatts (kWh)	
kWhs Used for Billing Period			
Customers Charge for Basic Service			6.79
Electric Energy Charge	0.13444	989	
State Tax			0.29
Total Electric Charge			
Electric Charge--Previous Year			
Year of 1995	ACTUAL USAGE	ESTIMATED USAGE	
MAY	480	493	
JUNE	590	640	
JULY	998	876	
AUGUST	1007	996	
SEPTEMBER	923	923	
OCTOBER	754	823	
NOVEMBER	560	632	
DECEMBER	578	632	
JANUARY	589	550	
FEBRUARY	601	598	
MARCH	530	530	
APRIL	510	520	

Rate GR Gas General Service Residential			
from: September 27, 1996			
to: October 26, 1996			
Meter Number 015-87-5467			
Ccf Used for Billing Period			
Gas Charge			
Customers Charge for Basic Service			8.54
Gas Energy Charge	1.334	91	
State Tax			0.32
Total Gas Charge			
Gas Charge--Previous Year			
Year of 1995--Ccf	ACTUAL USAGE	ESTIMATED USAGE	
MAY	61	62	
JUNE	62	60	
JULY	60	67	
AUGUST	58	64	
SEPTEMBER	74	72	
OCTOBER	81	86	
NOVEMBER	86	94	
DECEMBER	99	97	
JANUARY	110	112	
FEBRUARY	116	107	
MARCH	94	95	
APRIL	63	66	

2. Enter a formula to compute the Electric Energy Charge for the month from September 27 to October 26, 1996.
3. Enter a formula to compute Total Electric Charge which would include the basic service, the Energy Charge, and the State Tax.
4. Enter a formula to compute the Gas Energy Charge for the same period.
5. Enter a formula to compute the Total Gas Charge which would include basic service, the Gas Energy Charge, and State Tax. SAVE AS: ELECTRIC.
6. Create a column chart which illustrates the ACTUAL USAGE and the ESTIMATED USAGE for electric for the previous year of 1995.
7. The months will be the X-axis and the values will be the Y-axis.
8. Enter a chart title, legends and data labels.
9. Embed the chart on the spreadsheet.
10. Print the spreadsheet and the chart.
11. Create another column chart which illustrates the ACTUAL USAGE and the ESTIMATED USAGE for gas.
12. Enter a chart title, legends and data labels. Embed the gas energy chart underneath the electric chart. (This may require some sizing of the charts).
13. SAVE AS: ELECTRIC. Print the spreadsheet with both graphs embedded.

Competencies:

After completing this unit, you will know how to:

1. Create a pie, line, bar, etc. chart
2. Enter legends and titles on a chart
3. Embed the chart on a spreadsheet
4. Enter a chart on a separate page
5. Enter data labels on a chart
6. Enhance the chart with fonts, color
7. Enter an X and Y axis title
8. Size the graph
9. Change the Y-axis scale
10. Chart with one or multiple value variables
11. Change the type of chart

UNIT 13

Concepts:

Advanced Spreadsheets
Accounting Worksheets
Financial Statements
Cell Reference
Copying a Spreadsheet to a separate file

Points to Remember:

- Financial Statements contain several parts.
- Cell reference means that one cell simply refers to the value (not the formula) in another cell.
- Ranges can be copied as the calculated values not as the formula.
- When copying to another file, all formulas may need to be changed to range values in order to copy them to another file.
- There will be negatives in some spreadsheets in this unit.
- Optional blank grids are available in the back of this book for use with these spreadsheets.

Exercise 102 - Advanced Spreadsheet, Financial Statements

SAVE AS: WYLIES

Wylies Inc. is compiling the data for its 1996 financial statements. There are four parts to a financial statement: the *income statement*, the *beginning balance sheet*, the *ending balance sheet*, and the *cash flow statement*. The purpose of these financial statements are to evaluate the financial status of the business. To compute the cash flow statements, you must refer back to the income statement and the balance sheets.

HELPFUL HINTS

- ➔ Enter the values in B5, B6, etc. as negatives.
- ➔ To compute the 1996 Net Income, Total Assets, Total Liabilities, etc. simply add the values in their area.
- ➔ To compute changes in Accounts Receivable and Inventory, subtract December from January but to compute changes in Accounts Payable, subtract January from December.
- ➔ The ending cash flow balance on the cash flow statement should equal the cash per Dec 31, 1996 balance sheet.

Directions

1. Enter the spreadsheet as shown.
2. Enter all numbers in parentheses as negative numbers and format as shown.
3. Enter a function in cell B10 to show 1996 NET INCOME.
4. Enter a function in cell B19 to show Total Assets of the Opening Balance.
5. Enter a function in B27 to show Total Liabilities and Owner's Equity.
6. Enter a function in B35 to show Total Assets and in B43 to Show Total Liabilities.
7. In cell B41 use a cell reference to refer to cell B10. In B46 use a cell reference to reflect opening statement *cash. Type =B15 or +B15. Do not type 4000.*
8. In cell B47 use a cell reference to refer to cell B41 (1996 Net Income).
9. In cell B48 enter a formula to show the change in Accounts Receivable. Hint: January-December.

10. In cell B49 enter a formula to show the change in Inventory from January to December.
11. In cell B50 enter a formula to show the change in Accounts Payable. This is computed differently than Inventory and Accounts Receivable.
12. Enter a function in B52 to show December 31, 1996 cash balance.
13. Format all values as currency.
14. SAVE AS: WYLIES and print.

	A	B
1	**WYLIE'S INCORPORATED**	
2		
3	**1996 INCOME STATEMENT**	
4	SALES	$80,000
5	COST OF SALES	($30,000)
6	SALARIES	($10,000)
7	ADVERTISING	($8,000)
8	OTHER	($6,000)
9		
10	1996 NET INCOME	
11		
12		
13	**Beginning Balance Sheet**	
14	ASSETS	JAN 1 1996
15	CASH	$4,000
16	ACCOUNTS RECEIVABLE	$3,000
17	INVENTORY	$8,000
18		
19	TOTAL ASSETS	
20		
21		
22	LIABILITIES AND OWNERS EQUITY	
23	ACCOUNTS PAYABLE	$7,000
24	OWNER'S EQUITY AT JAN 1	$8,000
25	1996 NET INCOME	$0
26		
27	TOTAL LIABILITIES AND OWNERS EQUITY	
28		
29	**Ending Balance Sheet**	
30	ASSETS	DEC 31 1996
31	CASH	$25,000
32	ACCOUNTS RECEIVABLE	$7,000
33	INVENTORY	$6,000
34		
35	TOTAL ASSETS	
36		
37		
38	LIABILITIES AND OWNERS EQUITY	
39	ACCOUNTS PAYABLE	$4,000
40	OWNER'S EQUITY AT JAN 1	$8,000
41	1996 NET INCOME	$26,000
42		
43	TOTAL LIABILITIES AND OWNERS EQUITY	
44		
45	**1996 CASH FLOW STATEMENT**	
46	CASH BALANCE	
47	1996 NET INCOME	
48	CHANGE IN ACCOUNTS RECEIVABLE	
49	CHANGE IN INVENTORY	
50	CHANGE IN ACCOUNTS PAYABLE	
51		
52	DECEMBER 31, 1996 CASH BALANCE	

Exercise 103 - Advanced Spreadsheet, Payroll

SAVE AS: PAYDAY

Kiddee Toy Company is computing the gross pay for its employees for the week ending July 26, 1996. All the employees in the payroll statement are full time employees and receive a salary based on a 40 hour week. The employees receive time and a half of their hourly rate for any hours worked over 40 hours. They also receive double their hourly rate for any holiday hours worked.

Directions

1. Enter the information into a spreadsheet.
2. Enter a formula in the column SALARY 40 HOURS to show each employee's base salary based on a 40 hour week.
3. Create an "If" statement for OVERTIME HOURS. If hours worked are over 40 then subtract 40 from hours worked. If the hours worked are not over 40, put a 0 (zero) in the cell.
4. Enter a formula in a separate column to compute OVERTIME PAY.
5. Enter a formula in a separate column for HOLIDAY PAY. HINT: Employees receive double their hourly pay for each holiday hour worked.
6. Enter a formula for GROSS PAY. This is based on SALARY, OVERTIME PAY, and HOLIDAY PAY.
7. Copy all formulas appropriately.
8. Enter a formula for TOTAL GROSS PAY paid by the KIDDEE TOY COMPANY.
9. Format all values as shown.
10. SAVE AS: PAYDAY.
11. Print in landscape with gridlines in compressed print.
12. Using the database capabilities, set the criteria range to search for all employees making more than $350 gross pay. Use the entire spreadsheet as the input range and include all fields in the output range of your choice.
13. Print it on a separate page.

KIDDEE TOY COMPANY
PAYROLL FOR WEEK ENDING JULY 26. 1996

EMPLOYEE	HOURLY RATE	HOURS WORKED	SALARY 40 HOURS	OVERTIME HOURS	OVERTIME PAY	HOLIDAY HOURS	HOLIDAY PAY	GROSS PAY
TOM JOHNSON	$15.90	52				8		
AL BROWN	$11.75	43				0		
SUE THOMAS	$14.90	61				16		
TIA RAMON	$9.50	54				8		
VINCE RAGETTI	$10.00	47				0		
TANYA WOOD	$15.65	40				0		
DARNELL ALBERT	$9.87	41				16		
BRAD LUMBERG	$12.76	56				8		
PAT GRIPE	$9.90	65				0		
JOHN A. DOLHEFER	$13.76	44				8		
KATHY SHUG	$11.75	46				16		
LISA FILIGITTI	$15.65	51				8		
TED HOLIBAK	$10.50	40				0		
PAM McCABE	$12.75	50				0		
MIKE O'DONNELL	$14.10	47				16		
RAY LINDSEY	$10.25	53				8		

Notes:

Exercise 104 - Advanced Spreadsheet, Travel Expenses

SAVE AS: TRAVELOG

Mark R. Meyes, as executive vice president of Wylies Incorporated, will be traveling across the United States meeting with corporate advisors from three of their other corporate offices. Company policy requires that Mark keep a very accurate account of his travel expenses. Mark will pay for the trip and then he will be reimbursed by the company. He will be traveling from Monday, August 5, to Wednesday, August 7, 1996.

Directions

1. Use the information below to create a spreadsheet for a travel log.
2. Mark had traveled for 3 days – Monday, Tuesday, and Wednesday.
3. On Monday, he drove 330 miles; on Tuesday, he drove 280; and on Wednesday, he drove 550 miles.
4. He receives 32 cents per mile.
5. His parking and toll expenses per day were as follows: Monday, $27; Tuesday, $34 and Wednesday, $42.
6. His lodging expenses were as follows: Monday, $145; Tuesday, $174; and Wednesday, $123.
7. His total food expenses were as follows: Monday, $112; Tuesday, $141; and Wednesday, $157.
8. He received $3 for each phone call. He made 5 calls total; two on Monday and Tuesday and 1 on Wednesday.
9. Other expenses such as seminar fees, etc., were as follows: Monday, $55; Tuesday, $101; and Wednesday, $41.
10. The expense report should have each expense for each day of the week.
11. Enter a formula to show TOTAL for all three days.
12. Format cells accordingly.
13. Enhance spreadsheet with bold, underline, font changes, etc.
14. Create a pie chart to show percent of each expense with legends and a chart title. HINT: This may require moving information. Do not include totals in the chart.
15. Embed the chart on the spreadsheet.
16. SAVE AS: TRAVELOG.
17. Print the chart with the spreadsheet.

Notes:

 Exercise 105 - Advanced Spreadsheet

SAVE AS: FORECAST

Every June, the Kiddee Toy Company does a Projection of Sales for the upcoming Christmas season. The 1996 Projection Forecast of Sales is based on the sales increases or decreases from 1994 to 1995.

This spreadsheet will be used to compute the increase or decrease in sales from 1994 to 1995 and 1996 Projected Sales. If the sales decreased from 1994 levels, the owner will purchase the same number in 1996 as in 1995. The owner, Marsha Johnson, has decided to buy 7% more of each item that had an increase. It is crucial to have sufficient inventory to keep up with the demand of each popular item.

Directions

1. Create a spreadsheet with the following information:

KIDDEE TOY COMPANY
FORECAST ANALYSIS FOR CHRISTMAS 1996

ITEM	UNIT SALES 1994	UNIT SALES 1995	INCREASE OR DECREASE	PROJECTED SALES 1996
OLIVIA	10000	12000		
HOT SHOTS	5500	6200		
SPEED WHEELS	1200	1400		
ROBOTIC ZAK	22000	22100		
VEGA GAME SYSTEMS	18000	23000		
BABY SURPRISE	4500	5600		
OOZY MONSTER	3700	3650		
TECH KITCHEN	2900	4590		
MONTANA TRAIL	3800	4200		
ELECTRIC MAN	19000	13000		
VIRTUAL MORTALITY	24500	31000		
MAGIC STONES	1650	940		
DRAWING INTENSITY	988	520		
OLIVIA'S PLAYHOUSE	1287	1780		

2. Enter a formula to compute the increase or decrease in sales from 1994 to 1995.
3. To compute Projected Sales, enter an "If" statement. If there was an increase in unit sales from 1994 to 1995, compute a 7% increase of 1995 Projected Sales. HINT: Remember to not only multiply the percents but to add the base year of 1995 for the total Projected Sales. If the unit sales did not increase from 1994 to 1995 then order the same unit sales as in 1995.
4. Change the fonts, row height, and underline the items that have an increase.
5. Sort from highest to lowest Projected Sales.
6. Create a Header and Footer of your choice.
7. Create a pie chart based on Projected Sales.
8. Embed the pie chart on the spreadsheet.
9. SAVE AS: FORECAST.
10. Print the chart and spreadsheet.

Exercise 106 - Advanced Spreadsheet, Checkbook

SAVE AS: CHECKBOO

An electronic spreadsheet can be used to keep a running balance of checking accounts for individuals or companies. To compute a running balance, start with the ending balance, add deposits and subtract withdrawals and checks. Always add or subtract from the previous balance. Enter the check amounts and withdrawals separately.

Directions

1. Enter the following information into the spreadsheet.

MATTHEW'S CHECKING ACCOUNT

CHECK NUMBER	DATE	PAYOR	AMOUNT
876	Feb 4, 1996	Telephone Co.	$54.67
877	Feb 7, 1996	Macon Appliance	$786.54
878	Feb 7, 1996	H & T Water Inc.	$82.90
879	Feb 16, 1996	Lacy's Dept. Store	$121.88
880	Feb. 21, 1996	Olympic Mortgage	$785.50
881	Feb 21, 1996	Springfield Electric	$142.65
882	March 2, 1996	A & A Auto Service	$425.25
883	March 4, 1996	Village Meats	$37.86
884	March 9, 1996	Telephone Co.	$66.21
885	March 9, 1996	Dr. Repice	$40.00
886	March 9, 1996	Holy Trinity Church	$20.00
887	March 18, 1996	Village Meats	$16.50
888	March 22, 1996	Olympic Mortgage	$785.50
889	March 24, 1996	Springfield Electric	$128.99
890	April 4, 1996	I.M. Healed Drug Store	$52.22
891	April 7, 1996	C & S Electronics	$41.41
892	April 8, 1996	Telephone Co.	$69.69
893	April 10, 1996	Holy Trinity Church	$20.00
894	April 11, 1996	Dr. Repice	$40.00

2. The beginning balance was $1,876 on February 4, 1996, before any check was written.
3. In addition to the checks listed, the following deposits were made into this checking account: February 9, $250; February 27, $900; March 12, $1300; April 9, $300.
4. The following were withdrawals: March 3, $100; March 20, $300; and March 31, $250.
5. Enter all the above information into the spreadsheet to show the running balance of the checkbook.
6. Enter *one* formula to show the balance on February 4, 1996, of $1,876 that will subtract each check and each withdrawal and add each deposit. HINT: *The formula will give your checkbook balance on any given day.*
7. Only enter one formula and copy.
8. How much money is in the checking account at the end of April 11, 1996 after the check to Dr. Repice has been made?
9. SAVE AS: CHECKBOO.
10. Print in compressed print to fit on one page.

Exercise 107- Advanced Spreadsheet

SAVE AS: BENEFITS

For most companies, the cost of offering benefits to employees is extremely expensive. If an employee makes $15.90 as an hourly wage, the company also pays an additional cost for benefits. Some benefits are based on percent and some are specific amounts. This spreadsheet will not only show the hourly wage but the amount that the company pays for *all benefits* for *each* employee.

A benefits analysis will be performed for each employee of the Kiddee Toy Company. This company would like to compute the total per hour salary plus all amounts Kiddee Toy Company pays for benefits per employee.

Directions

1. Open the file PAYDAY and copy columns A and B to a new file as a range value.
2. Save the new file as BENEFITS.
3. Close PAYDAY. Enter the following information into a spreadsheet in columns C, D and E. Columns A and B will be a reference for per hour pay.

	A	B	C	D	E
1			BENEFITS ANALYSIS		
2					
3			PAY PER HOUR	$15.90	
4					
5			BENEFIT		TOTAL
6					
7			VACATION	4%	
8			SICK LEAVE	2%	
9			PENSION	5%	
10			SOCIAL SECURITY	7%	
11			UNEMPLOYMENT	0.5%	
12			401 K	4%	
13					
14			TOTAL		
15					
16			HEALTH INSURANCE		
17			DENTAL INSURANCE		
18					
19			TOTAL PER HOUR BENEFITS PAID		
20			PAY PER HOUR plus BENEFITS PAID		

4. The per hour rate plus the benefits per hour paid is what it costs the company to employ Tom.
5. The $15.90 reflects the hourly rate of Tom Johnson.
6. Using PAY PER HOUR as an absolute cell, enter a formula in E7 to compute the 7% of the pay per hour that the company contributes for vacation pay. HINT: pay per hour will be an absolute for all formulas with percents.
7. Enter a formula to compute the amount the company contributes for sick leave, pension, social security, unemployment, and the 401K plan.
8. The health insurance is not a percent. The company pays $1.10 per hourly rate for each employee's health benefits. Enter $1.10 in cell E16.
9. The dental insurance is also not a percent. The company pays $.62 cents per hourly rate. Enter the value in E17.
10. Enter a formula for TOTAL PER HOUR BENEFITS PAID.
11. Enter a formula for PAY PER HOUR plus BENEFITS PAID.
12. RESAVE AS: BENEFITS.
13. Print.
14. Change the value of $15.90 in D3 to reflect Al Brown's hourly rate of $11.75.
15. All formulas should have changed to reflect that new value entered.
16. Print.
17. Enter a benefits analysis for Lisa Filgitti and Pam McCabe and print but do not resave.
18. SAVE AS: BENEFITS.
19. Print.

Competencies:

After completing this unit, you will know how to:

1. Create advanced spreadsheets
2. Create financial statements
3. Create payroll statements
4. Create a running balance in a checkbook

UNIT 14

Concepts:

Advanced Spreadsheet
Integrated Software
Word Processing Application
Graphics Application
Spreadsheet Application
Database Application

Points to Remember:

- Always save before cutting and pasting from one software package to another.
- Make all format changes *before* cutting and pasting.
- Insert rows before inserting graphics because the graphics will insert on top of text.

Exercise 108 - Integrated Project Spreadsheet and Graphics Application

SAVE AS: PAYDAY2

In the file Payday the Gross Pay was calculated by computing the Salary based on 40 hours and adding Overtime pay (employees are paid time and a half) and Holiday pay (employees are paid double time). To compute Net Pay, add all the deductions and subtract them from the Gross Pay.

Directions

1. Retrieve PAYDAY.
2. Insert a blank column B.
3. Cut and paste the GROSS PAY column and move the contents into column B as values.
4. Copy columns A and B to a new file. HINT: You cannot do a *regular* copy; it must be copied as a range value.
5. Save the new file as PAYDAY2.
6. Close PAYDAY.
7. In PAYDAY2, create a *separate* column for each of the following deductions:

Social Security Tax	6.2%
Federal Withholding Tax	15%
Medicare	1.45%
State Tax	2.8%
401K	5%

8. Enter a formula in each column to compute the deduction for each and copy down.
9. Enter a formula to compute TOTAL DEDUCTIONS.
10. Enter a formula to show NET PAY.
11. Sort in descending order on NET PAY.
12. Change the fonts, row height, shading, etc.
13. Import a graphic from a graphics application. Choose a relevant picture.
14. SAVE AS: PAYDAY2 and print the spreadsheet and the graphic.

KIDDEE TOY COMPANY
PAYROLL FOR WEEK ENDING JULY 26. 1996

EMPLOYEE	GROSS PAY	S.S.T.	F.W.T.	MEDICARE	STATE TAX	401K	TOTAL DEDUCTIONS	NET PAY
TOM JOHNSON								
AL BROWN								
SUE THOMAS								
TIA RAMON								
VINCE RAGETTI								
TANYA WOOD								
DARNELL ALBERT								
BRAD LUMBERG								
PAT GRIPE								
JOHN A. DOLHEFER								
KATHY SHUG								
LISA FILIGITTI								
TED HOLIBAK								
PAM McCABE								
MIKE O'DONNELL								
RAY LINDSEY								

Notes:

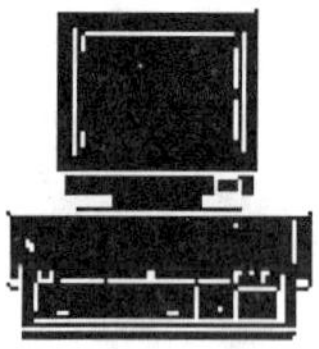

Exercise 109 - Integrated Project Spreadsheet with Embedded Chart and Graphic Application

SAVE AS: COMPUTER

Computer Concepts has stores in four states: Pennsylvania, North Carolina, California, and Texas. They recently discovered that because of increased salary and overhead, they have had a decrease in profit. After much discussion they realize that they must close *one* of these four stores.

You will decide which store will close by choosing the *one* who had the lowest percent of increase in sales from 1995 to 1996. *Remember this decision is not based on Actual Sales but the percent of increase and who had the lowest total increase.*

Directions

1. Enter the following information into a spreadsheet.

Lancaster, Pennsylvania
ACTUAL SALES

Quarter	1995 Sales	1996 Sales
First Quarter	612,990	611,989
Second Quarter	767,876	794,230
Third Quarter	797,542	802,454
Fourth Quarter	834,787	832,009

Raleigh, North Carolina
ACTUAL SALES

Quarter	1995 Sales	1996 Sales
First Quarter	522,690	531,211
Second Quarter	541,487	567,170
Third Quarter	576,319	567,222
Fourth Quarter	603,651	631,877

San Francisco, California
ACTUAL SALES

Quarter	1995 Sales	1996 Sales
First Quarter	789,409	790,221
Second Quarter	777,347	732,110
Third Quarter	802,139	807,392
Fourth Quarter	820,321	829,997

Austin, Texas
ACTUAL SALES

Quarter	1995 Sales	1996 Sales
First Quarter	544,987	509,342
Second Quarter	567,007	580,002
Third Quarter	601,131	607,995
Fourth Quarter	611,161	639,998

2. Enter formulas for each state and each quarter to compute the following:

   - Increase or decrease from 1995 sales to 1996 sales per quarter.
   - TOTAL increase or decrease for the year.
   - The percent of the increase or decrease.
   - The TOTAL percent of the increase or decrease for the year.

3. Import an applicable graphic from a graphic application and embed it on the spreadsheet. Hint: Use a picture relevant to a computer.
4. Create four separate column charts to illustrate the quarter and the percent of the increase or decrease per quarter – do not include the totals.
5. Embed all four charts on the spreadsheet.
6. Which store are you going to close?
7. Which store had the highest increase in sales from 1995 to 1996?
8. SAVE AS: COMPUTER.
9. Print the spreadsheet and all of the charts.

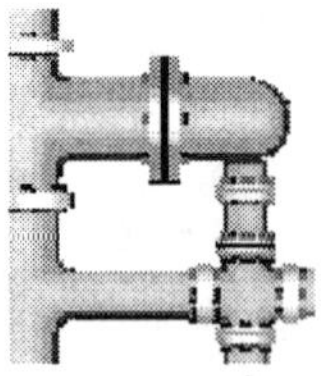

Exercise 110 - Integrated Project Word Processing, Spreadsheet and Graphic Application

SAVE AS: Flood

Vanessa woke up early one morning to feed the baby. When she went downstairs to get the baby's bottle, she noticed a considerable amount of water on the family room rug–about a bucket or two. She and Michael tried to find where the water was coming from but their attempt was futile.

The next day, the plumber informed them that a pipe from the shower on the second floor had burst and that the damage was extensive to the second floor bathroom and the first floor family room.

Vanessa called her homeowners insurance company, Mystate, and they sent an adjuster to inspect the damage. He developed a draft which represents assessment of the damages to the first floor family room and the second floor bathroom.

As the insurance adjuster, you must subtract the depreciation cost from the value of the damaged wallpaper and paint. For the new items to be installed, you must calculate replacement value. You will need three types of software applications to enter this information.

Directions

1. This project will contain three parts: (1) a letter from the insurance adjuster; (2) a spreadsheet with estimates of the cash value loss to the family room and the bathroom; (3) and a graphic (picture) embedded on both the letter and the spreadsheet.
2. As the insurance adjuster, retype the letter on the next page explaining the settlement in a word processing software document.
3. When you have finished typing the letter in a word processing application, import a graphic of your choice from a graphic application on the letter.
4. Size the picture (graphic) accordingly on the letter.
5. Save the letter as FLOOD.

MYSTATE INSURANCE COMPANY
1000 Kennedy Way
Philadelphia, PA 19002
October 25, 1996

Michael and Vanessa Chateau
112 Florence Drive
Newtown Square, PA 19073

Dear Mr. And Mrs. Chateau:

We are enclosing a draft which represents payment of the building loss on an actual cash value basis (acv). This draft includes a copy of the estimate of the damages.

The policy provides building replacement cost coverage. You may make an additional claim within 180 days after the date of loss for an additional payment under this coverage.

To make an additional claim, please contact me to schedule a re–inspection.

Thank you for your cooperation in concluding this loss.

Sincerely,

Anthony L. Martelli
Claim Specialist

6. Enter the following information into a spreadsheet.

FAMILY ROOM

DESCRIPTION	QUANTITY	UNIT COST	DEPRECIATION	CASH VALUE
paint the ceiling—two coats	233 square feet	.36	16.77	
wallpaper—premium grade	384 square feet	2.00	125.99	
prep wall for wallpaper	384 square feet	.26		
carpet pad	25.5 sq. yds.	3.86		
carpet	25.5 sq. yds	32.45		
detach and reset carpet	25.5 sq. yds	4.20		
repair drywall and patch		285		

BATHROOM

DESCRIPTION	CASH VALUE
remove tile, shower door and pan	200
wonder board and retile shower	560
repair drywall	185
install new trap and supplies	357
plumber's estimate for labor	978

7. Enter both estimates on the same spreadsheet in two different areas.
8. Compute the Total estimate for the family room.
9. Compute the Total estimate for the bathroom.
10. Create a formula to compute the Total estimate of both rooms.
11. Embed a graphic of your choice on the top of the spreadsheet.
12. SAVE AS: FLOOD1.
13. Embed the spreadsheet containing both estimates and the graphic on the second page of the letter.
14. RESAVE the letter as: FLOOD.
15. Print the entire project.

Notes:

Exercise 111 - Integrated Project Word Processing, Spreadsheet, Graphic and Database Applications

SAVE AS: ANALYSIS

A stock or mutual fund portfolio represents all of the investments made by one individual or one firm. This portfolio can be chosen by the investor with the assistance of a stockbroker or financial advisor. Sometimes mutual funds will charge a *load (fee)*. The calculated load amount is subtracted from the total cost.

A pie graph, which is always based on 100%, will give a clear picture of the total investment (*percent* of each investment). A column or stacked bar graph will display the *growth* of *each* investment.

Directions

1. Create a spreadsheet to show a portfolio for Prescott Sims with the following information:

MUTUAL FUND	TOTAL COST	LOAD	LOAD AMOUNT	NET AMOUNT INVESTED	PROJECTED INCREASE	PROJECTED GAIN	NET VALUE
BENNINGS	$5,000.00	3%			6%		
CORE FUNDS	$2,300.00	2%			2%		
EXPLORERS GROWTH	$1,800.00	2%			5%		
DILWORTH FUNDS	$9,500.00	0%			10%		
DISCOVERS	$1,200.00	1%			2%		
MERRIETTA GROWTH	$2,300.00	0%			4%		
TRAVELS INTNL.	$3,100.00	3%			5%		
BINGEMTON FUNDS	$1,100.00	2%			22%		

2. Enter a formula for Load Amount and Net Amount Invested.
3. Create another formula to compute Projected Gain Amount.
4. Compute Net Value.
5. Change fonts, row height, etc.
6. SAVE AS: ANALYSIS.

7. As the stockbroker, write a letter to Prescott Sims, 78 Riser Street, New York, NY to explain the total investments, load fee and projected gain. Sign the letter as yourself.
8. Embed the spreadsheet on the letter.
9. Embed a graphic on the letter.
10. SAVE the letter as: ANALYSI2.
11. As the stockbroker you also would like to create a database of Prescott Sims' investments.
12. The Transaction Fee is not the same as the load fee. It is an additional fee.
13. Include the following information in the database.

MUTUAL FUND	TOTAL COST	FUND CATEGORY	TRANSACTION FEE	FUND MANAGER	DATE INVESTED
BENNINGS	$5,000	Aggressive	Yes	Heiko Chou	8/15/96
CORE FUNDS	$2,300	Growth	No	Tina Lipper	8/15/96
EXPLORERS GROWTH	$1,800	Balanced Income	Yes	Jamal Brown	9/5/96
DILWORTH FUNDS	$9,500	Global Equity	Yes	Roy Hickler	8/15/96
DISCOVERS	$1,200	Balanced Income	Yes	Rick Plain	9/11/96
MERRIETTA GROWTH	$2,300	Aggressive	No	W. H. Camps	9/11/96
TRAVELS INTNL.	$3,100	Balanced Income	No	Alexa Holmes	8/15/96
BINGEMTON FUNDS	$1,100	Growth	Yes	Zak Harvey	9/5/96

14. Save the database as ANALYSI3.
15. Print all parts of the project.

Competencies:

After completing this unit, you will know how to:

1. Create an advanced spreadsheet
2. Import a graphic into a spreadsheet
3. Import a graphic into a word processing document
4. Import a spreadsheet into a word processing document
5. Enter information into a database related to a spreadsheet

	A	B	C	D	E	F	G	H
1								
2								
3								
4								
5								
6								
7								
8								
9								
10								
11								
12								
13								
14								
15								
16								
17								
18								
19								
20								
21								
22								
23								
24								
25								
26								
27								

Notes: